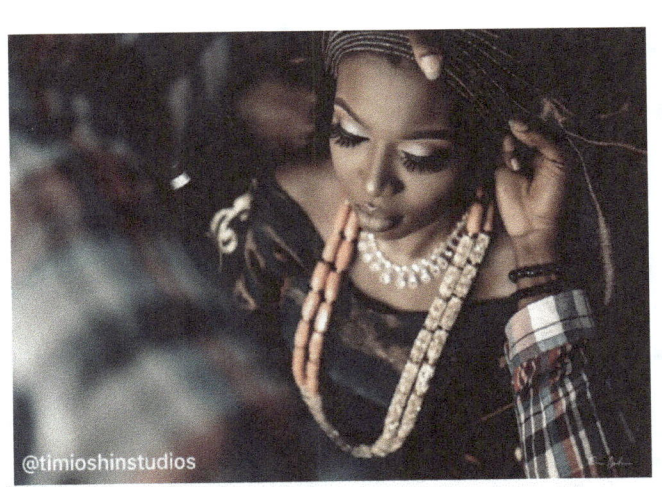

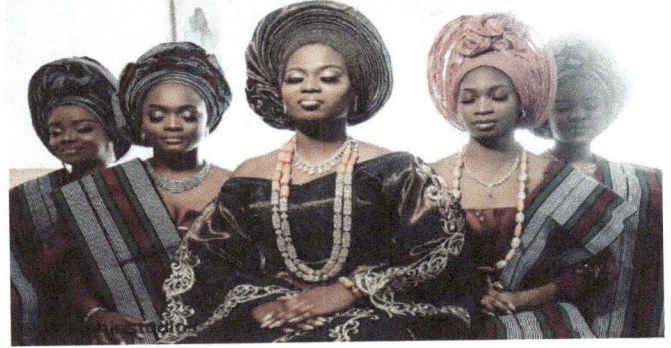

MORE THAN A WRAP

Fatola Eniola

Copyright © 2022 Eniola Fatola

All rights reserved.

ISBN.13: 979-8-7995-5700-3

DEDICATION

To all the people who have helped me become:

The folks who raised me – Olabode & Olufisayo Jolaogun.

And my vast extended family,

My circle of strong men and women, who always lifts me up,

My loyal and dedicated customers, fans and student all around the world who continue to make me proud

---

To God my creator who is the reason for my existence.

CONTENTS

Acknowledgments
Introduction ix
Preface x

1 Chapter 1   1

(GELE IN AFRICA: HISTORY & IMPORTANCE)

2 Chapter 2   14

(THE AESTHETICS OF GELE IN NIGERIAN EVENTS: DISCUSSING ASOEBI AND OWANBE)

3 Chapter 3   28

(TYPES OF GELE AND THE ROLES THEY PLAY)

4 Chapter 4   35

THE SOCIO-CULTURAL IMPORTANCE OF GELE IN AFRICA

5 Chapter 5   48

AFRICAN GELE IN OTHER PARTS OF THE WORLD: A PROGNOSIS

6 Chapter 6   64

THE FUTURE OF HEADWRAP CULTURE IN AFRICA AND THE WORLD AT LARGE

7 Chapter 7   77

HOW TO BE AN EXCEPTIONAL GELE STYLIST/ WORKSHOP

MORE THAN A WRAP

ACKNOWLEDGMENTS

A very big thank you to the Almighty God; my parents, Mr & Mrs. Jolaogun, HER; Erelu Bisi Fayemi; Dr. Oreofe Williams; Dr. Ade Adeseke; Mr. Feso Adegoroye Oyebade; Ojo Oluwasegun David (MOTIS); Amanna Chidinma, my editor; Tolu Adedara (ONIGELE); PHOTONIMI and everyone else who helped in the course of this book.
I pray the good Lord to bless and reward you abundantly.

MORE THAN A WRAP

INTRODUCTION

The rich culture of Africa hasn't all been contained in books, culture like art has so many diversities in topics that encompasses histories, folklore, traditions, artifacts, fashion, and lots more. In the world today, the majority of Africans who wear headwraps have little or no understanding about it, merely seeing it as just a fashion statement. This book brings to illumination histories and tradition that has not been taught in schools but of which would be great benefits to the reader and the world at large.

With overwhelming excitement, I would be taking you on a tour around one of the most popular crafts in Africa, known for its distinction in adding beauty and value to Africa women.

A WRAP THAT TELLS A STORY.

MORE THAN A WRAP

PREFACE

The drive behind the composition of this book is to fill the void of knowledge regarding the cultural meaning, aesthetical values, religious beliefs, and as well historical references of headwraps around the world. In the bid of gathering expository and quality information, few data were gotten from the net as there are no books or journals contained with this information.

As a professional headwrap stylist and enthusiast, also a first-degree holder in arts, I have been able to put together this beautiful piece.

As the author this book, I would like to urge readers around the world to quit hesitation and dive into this wealth of information and knowledge contained in this book and also share it with friends and family. This book is also recommended for learning in educational and technical institutions around the world.

1 CHAPTER
GELE IN AFRICA: HISTORY AND IMPORTANCE

The African culture is diverse and fascinating. Africa houses many cultures. Each African country has its cultural distinction, language, and ethnicity, and in this book, we will explore a few of these tribes and cultural arts and crafts.

The lack of resources (especially writing materials) caused African history to be passed orally, researchers had to depend on archaeology, scientific genetics, and oral history to determine Africa's history. In Africa, unlike Europe, history isn't stored in decaying buildings but it is found with the people found there. Egypt whose civilization was one of the first in Africa started recording its history, this spread to Nubia, Maghreb, and the Horn of Africa.

Definition of Art

Frist off let's start with "what is art?", Art is diverse and complex. Art as a philosophical concept has been debated overages, there hasn't been any agreement on a particular definition. Its luxurious nature dwells in an all-encompassing definition. Art is ever-changing, what is termed art at one period tends to grow as the discipline evolves. Fisher (1993), commented on the difficulty in creating a common definition for art.

He said, "The nature of art allows all the actors in the art fraternity -the audience, curators, editors, critics, art historians, and theorists- to play important role in determining the direction and definition of art".

According to (Marder, 2019), the term "art" is related to the Latin word "ars" meaning, art, skill, or craft. The first known use of the word comes from 13th-century manuscripts.

However, the word art and its many variants ("Artem", "Eart", etc.) have probably existed since the founding of Rome. Lumen learning defines Art as "a highly diverse range of human activities engaged in creating visual, auditory, or performed artifacts -artworks that express the author's imaginative or technical skill, and are intended to be appreciated for their beauty or emotional power."

The Expressiveness of Art

Ancient documented forms of art are visual arts, these are images or objects in fields like painting, sculpture, printmaking, photography, and other visual media. The architecture was seen as visual art, they considered the decorative arts that involve the creation of objects and were practical in a way that other visual arts weren't, like a painting.

Art can be characterized in terms of its representation of reality, mimesis; the expression, the communication of emotions, or other qualities. Though constitutes of art have been disputed over and changed from time to time. Generally, the descriptions of art center on the idea of imaginative or technical skills stemming from human creativity and skills. There is no single aesthetic trait or value in visually identifying a work of art. Consider a Baroque painting it does not share much in common with a contemporary performance piece, but both are seen as art.

Author of "The History of Art", H.W Janson said, "...we cannot escape viewing works of art in the context of time and circumstance, whether past or present. How indeed could it be otherwise, so long as the art is still being created all around us, opening our eyes almost daily to new experiences and thus forcing us to adjust our sights?"

From the 11th century to the end of the 17th century, art was seen as anything done skillfully in Western culture. Meaning artists were protective about their skills. Artists were free to paint in any genre and were allowed to earn from their work during the epitome of the Dutch Golden Age in the robust economic and cultural climate of 1700 in the

Netherlands.

Art may seem indefinable but there exist certain formal guidelines for its analysis and judgments. Lumen learning defines Formalism: as a concept in art theory in which an artwork's artistic value is determined solely by its form, or how it is made. Formalism evaluates works on a purely visual level, considering medium and compositional elements as opposed to any reference to realism, context, or content.

Quote from Henry James's short story, "The Middle Years", "We work in the dark — we do what we can — we give what we have. Our doubt is our passion and our passion is our task. The rest is the madness of art".

According to Aristotle (284-322 BC), "Art completes what nature can't bring to a finish. The artist gives us knowledge of nature's unrealized ends".

We can focus on a wider and more traditional concept of artistic properties that includes art in pan-cultural and trans-historical characteristics.

THE AFRICAN HEADWRAP

Headwraps are significant in African fashion and history, for their longevity and potent distinctive importance. It endured slavery and never went out of fashion. It is more than just a piece of fabric wound around the head.

An African "Head-wrap" is a piece of cloth tied around the head in a detailed and creative style. It is a strong cultural statement, a fashionable accessory, or a quick fit in styling one's hair.

Headwrap originated from sub-Saharan Africa and served specific functions for African women in the early 1700s, it has been a consistent feature in the lives of women for hundreds of years. Many queens, especially Nubian queens, adorned traditional headwear with beautiful flowers, elaborately woven with rich fabrics. Nigerian queens preferred lighter and finer materials especially special occasions, but Egyptian royalty had eyes for rock stunning, elaborate headdresses, regularly related to as powerful and inspirational.

The African women's Headwrap exhibits the features of sub-Saharan aesthetics and worldview, but early African women regarded Headwraps as a helmet of courage that evoked an image of their true homeland, Africa. They are seen as a uniform communal identity worn by millions of African women and their descendants, the African Headwrap has functioned as a symbol of beauty and power signifying absolute royalty.

Headwraps are specific to Africa and its diversified cultural group. In many societies, men and women have always worn various types of fabric on their heads. There appears to be culturally specific, the way the fabric is worn and the style in which the fabric is worn is the ultimate cultural marker. This "style" isn't particular to fashion, but a study of presenting oneself and how one ought to appear before others. In exploring this concept one must carefully note the importance of the design of Headwraps and the way it is styled by an African woman.

Headwraps being widely used by women, mostly elderly and married, head wraps represent one's social status and marital status. It is used for spiritual worship, elaborate ceremonial occasions, and recently, by younger women as a fashion accessory and a symbol of African pride and renaissance. If and when necessary, young women wear headwraps for cultural purposes.

HEADWRAP HISTORICAL BACKGROUND IN AFRICA

MORE THAN A WRAP

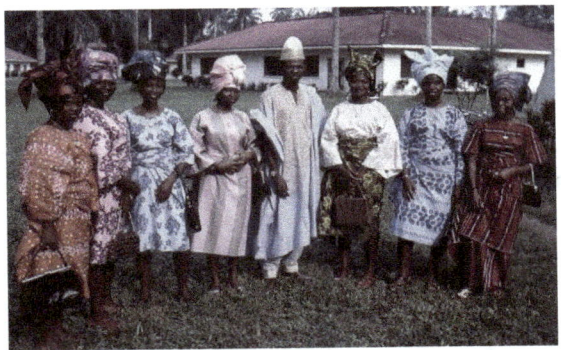

Its history can be traced back to the Nubia Empire and ancient Egypt. The wealthy and powerful adorned themselves with head wraps. Priests, kings, and queens often wore head wraps that were tall and had some sort of decoration such as sun disks or feathers. Head-warps were also used to identify a deity or god, the way it was styled and decorated.

Ancient Egypt and Nubia headwraps were worn by both sex, historians linked the wearing of headwraps as members of royalty in the times of pharaoh, where hieroglyphic evidence shows Pharaohs wearing headbands or covering their heads with wigs made from specific material to signify a specific meaning.

Headwraps are known by different names in different regions on the continent. In South Africa and Namibia head wraps are known as "doek", in Zimbabwe as "dhuku", in Botswana as "tuku" or "tukwi", in Malawi and Ghana as "duku", in Nigeria as "gele", and in Zambia as "chitambala".

One of the popular African Head-wrap is "Gele", which was found in West Africa. Geles are head garments with interesting colors, textures, patterns, and designs, it symbolizes much more than a head-wrap. Gele was a symbol of power and status in West Africa, often in exotic colors and styles, worn by those who could afford it. The headdress can serve as protection from the sun, for practicality.

The design and styles of head wraps continued to advance with time in West Africa, nowadays, headwraps found in West

Africa are seen as credible and authentic, they are tied up at the crown of the head.

In some parts of North Africa, the material used to make head coverings included beads, feathers, and shavings from the baobab tree. Headwrap born from slavery is now celebrated in African especially in the fashion industry to express style and identity.

HISTORY OF HEAD WRAP IN NIGERIA

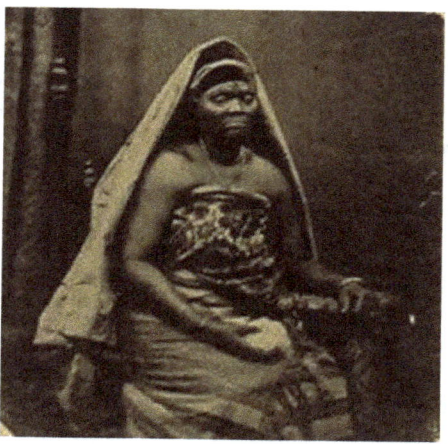

The Headwrap, "gele" (Yoruba word) in Nigeria, is most preferred large and elaborate. This is a flat piece of fabric mostly: Jean-like (Asooke), Starched Cotton fabric (Brocade), African Print, Paper-like fabric with plain or bold patterns (Sego, Jubilee, and more are some brand names of the paper-like fabric), heavily patterned Paper-like, Velvet-like fabric (Damask) and many more.

Geles are wrapped by hand to form a hat, they can be worn for day-to-day activities, visitations and even going to the market, but extravagant and ceremonial ones are worn to weddings, special events, church services, and other celebrations. Wearing gele is a tradition common to women in

Nigerian, especially to the Yoruba's and Igbos.

Geles, when worn, especially for big and elaborate events, it is typical they cover a woman's entire hair most times her ears too due to size and style of tying, leaving out her earrings on the lower part of her earlobes. The gele is usually worn in traditional attire that may or may not have the same pattern as the head-tie.

According to the Yorubas, the way a Gele is tied can indicate a woman's marital status. If a woman's gele's end is leaning to the right, it indicates she is married but if it is leaning to the left indicates she is Single. Nowadays, mostly in the urban areas, there isn't a defined indication of a Woman's marital status in the way she ties her gele. African Women are very particular on how they want their gele tied, like tied in levels for it to stand high, while some prefer tied more conservatively.

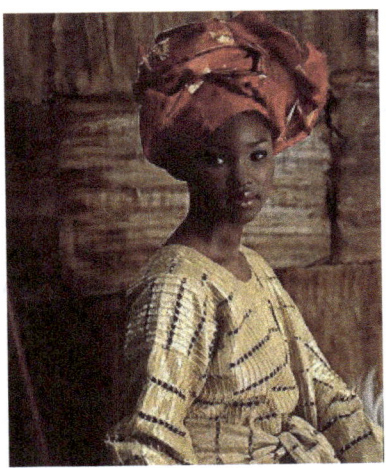

Gele being very beautiful and fascinating has gotten the attention of millions of people in different countries around the world. Many non-Africans wear gele as a sign of reverence when attending African events, some wear it as a part of their everyday fashion and some just have a soft spot for the Yoruba

Culture.

Traditionally, the style of gele varies throughout West and South African regions:

- Nigeria: women in this country has head wraps (gele) for every occasion: ceremonies (weddings, naming ceremony, etc.), church activities (Thanksgiving), feasts and important events, and just everyday activities. Gele is worn mostly on weekends.
- Ghana: women in this country wear head wraps on religious days (weekends), depending on their religion (Muslim, Seventh-Day Adventists, and Christian).
- Malawi: women in this country wear their head wraps in quite a conservative manner, majorly to protect their hair (during bad weather or when sleeping).
- South Africa: women in this country often wear white headwraps for church services or as an accessory.

Zimbabwe: women in this country wear head wraps as an accessory for creating a stylish look.

This black hair fashion has stood the test of time and space, despite the dispersal of African communities due to the Trans-Atlantic slave trade, emancipation, the Great Migration, and globalization. Headwraps links black women of the West with the traditions of their ancestors, and their cousins across the Atlantic.

The African Headwrap like a regal coronet draws the onlooker's gaze up, rather than down. The African women wear their Headwraps as a queen might wear a crown. The Headwrap corresponds to African women's manner of hairstyling; the hair is bounded up to expose the forehead and to a heightened mass on top of the head. These headwraps, "Gele", are worn by African Women to complement their African Attire it is usually the highlight of their appearance. A well-tied Gele can compensate for a not-so-great-looking outfit.

Meaning and Importance

MORE THAN A WRAP

The African Headwrap "Gele" is pronounced "gay-lay". Gele impresses by its various forms, twists, and perpendicular balances. The ritual meanings of gele may vary across regions, the simplest forms of gele look similar to a "bandana". The sophisticated designs require more effort and time, and they are produced from unique fabric produced specially for a gele.

Geles are spicy, a recipe in the African culture today simply because of their aesthetic value and as well cultural meaning and importance. Gele has a way of communicating a woman's social status depending on how it is tied, bogus ones could show how wealthy a person is or how fashion inclined a woman is, while the petite ones could mean simplicity. Importantly Gele is seen as a crown, which makes a woman feel like royalty though she might not be one.

HEADWRAP IN KENYA

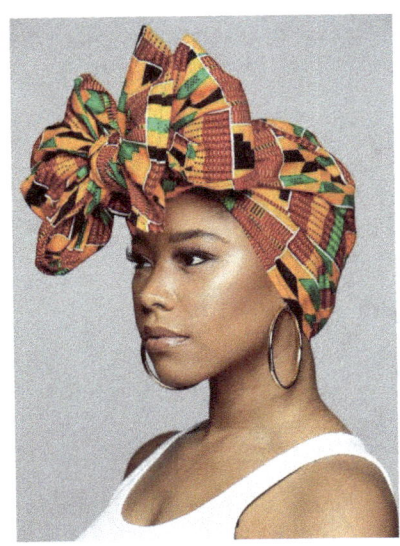

In Kenya, Headwraps are known as "Kilemba". The

Swahili coast of Kenya uses a lot of the Kanga and Kitenge fabrics as head and body wrap. Each culture in Kenya transforms wraps into a work of art. It takes time to wrap it in such intricate styles in any culture, they specialist this art which is a lucrative business.

Well-styled Kilemba is considered a masterpiece. Other popular Headwraps are the Sudanese's tagelmust and Tuareg turban, they are beautiful and long mostly men worn by man, there are many other cultural headwraps.

EGYPTIAN HEAD WRAP HISTORY

Ancient Egyptians cared about their appearance; they wore finely tailored and flattering clothes, they also greatly care about their bodies. Strangely, wealthy Egyptians—men and women— were bald. Copper razors found in tombs of upper-class Egyptians reveal the importance of being clean-shaven on the head and face, it was considered a sign of nobility. Archaeologists believe that the Egyptians shaved to keep themselves cool due to the hot Egyptian climate.

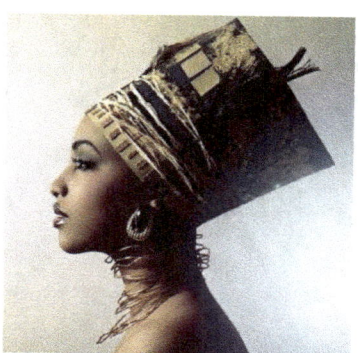

When you think of ancient Egyptian culture, you most likely picture pyramids or Sphinx, but what about those fancy headdresses that the gods and pharaohs wore. Headdresses, or crowns, are portrayed on statues, paintings, casket tops, and the death mask of ancient Egyptian history. These headdresses were elaborate, with gold and jewel accents, hieroglyphs, and pictures painted on them.

But what did they mean?

Symbols of Importance

Consider the possibility that the Egyptian headdress originated from their gods. Ancient Egyptian gods were originally displayed wearing headdresses to symbolize that they were mythical kings, even before creation. These set them apart from the common people in pictures and statues. The pharaohs of Egypt wore crowns during ceremonies, right from their coronation, to symbolize their closeness to the gods and their superiority to the people.

Types of Egyptian Headwrap

There were different colors for different regions of Egypt:
- Red crowns were used for pharaohs of Lower Egypt,
- White crowns were for pharaohs of Upper Egypt, and
- Blue crowns were for the pharaohs of the New Kingdom; like the crown, we often see on King Tut statues.

Some pharaohs could combine different crowns to be unique or to state some ceremonies more important than others. The death god, Osiris, had his crown no other god or pharaoh wore this crown, called the "Atef Crown" or "White Crown of Osiris", it was white and adorned on each side with feathers.

TRADITIONAL SIGNIFICANCE OF HEAD WARPS

In Yoruba, traditional headwraps indicate what a woman is; married, widowed, young, or old. Just from her head wrap, one could tell her status. Similarly, Southern African women were known to culturally wear 'Doeks' as an outward sign that they are engaged, married, or bereaved.

Headwraps signify different things in other cultures, like respect. In Zulu culture, women are expected to visit or appear before their in-laws with her head covered as a show of respect. In some parts of Xhosa women are also expected the same in 'Iqhiya'. In Sotho traditional wedding, in-laws give 'Makoti Ituku' to the bride as a sign that she has been accepted into their family.

RELIGION SIGNIFICANCE

In Islam, a Headwrap named turban is used for protection from sand and the desert sun, and it's also an element of spirituality. Colour also indicates the social position, for example, black represents those who consider themselves descendants of the Prophet Muhammad, therefore worn by very important Islamic leaders. In parts of the Persian Gulf, the turban has been replaced with a white or checker scarf, known as 'Keffiyeh'.

Many women consider wearing a turban or gele a cultural ritual: everything – from the way the hair is tied to the colors and the knots – means something. Lía Samantha said: "Our hair is an antenna that connects us with the universe, with that volatile energy that is dispersed, and the moment we decided to tie it inside a turban, what we are doing is wrapping that energy in a purpose. And the purpose is spiritual".

Part of the ritual is the tying of the knots (the art) is much like an inheritance, it is handed down from mother to daughter in many African communities. Knots are said to have special meaning: when the knot is on the side, it's synchronized with the location of the sun, while if it's tied three times, it signifies family: mother, father, and children.

Lía Samantha explains, "When we make the knot, we symbolize the union of yin and yang, good and evil, while when we wrap circularly we are emulating the movement of the Milky Way. The circular movement is the natural movement of the universe, and just like dreadlocks do in

Jamaica, we are elevating the spirit and telling God that we respect him".

CHAPTER 2

THE AESTHETICS OF GELE IN NIGERIAN EVENTS: DISCUSSING ASOEBI AND OWANBE

NIGERIA AND CULTURE

Nigeria is a country rich in culture and values, the majority of these culture has their festivals and celebrations. Nigeria's sophisticated cultural diversity makes it one of the most popular countries in Africa which has 527 languages with seven of them are extinct, it also has over 1150 dialects and ethnic groups. The six largest ethnic groups are the Hausa and Fulani in the north, the Igbo in the southeast, the Yoruba predominate in the southwest, the Tiv people of North Central Nigeria, and the Efik - Ibibio.

THE YORUBA CULTURE

The Yorubas ancient mythology is the most popular major in Nigeria. Its religion, claimed by its devotees, is said to be one of the oldest in the world and is still practiced today. Since it birth new and modified world religions such as Santería in Cuba and Candomblé in Brazil have sprung up.

The Yoruba ethnic group, "A people of rich soil and mystery" dance to the beats of the Batá drum under the moonlight, chanting to the Mother goddess "Iba'se Yemoja Olugbe-rere" (I give praise to you Yemoja, the one who brings goodness) and offering their gratitude to Oduduwa, the godfather of their land (this is a tribe with a story).

MORE THAN A WRAP

The Aso-Oke is the top of choice for gele – formally a textured, tightly hand-woven, glossy, cotton cloth crafted in different traditional patterns and colors. The fabric now often used is cotton, silk, rayon, and metallic lurex fibers. The result is a shiny, stiff fabric that is quality wrapping paper. Traditionally, Aso-Oke was a sign of wealth, it means "top cloth" and the Oba's (Nigeria's kings) preference.

History of The Yoruba Ethnic Group

The Yoruba ethnic group has over 40 million people inhabiting the southwestern and north-central regions of Nigeria, as well as southern and central Benin. Dating back to the transatlantic slave trade from 1500 to 1900, the Yoruba people also migrated to other countries, including Cuba, Dominican Republic, Brazil, Jamaica, Grenada, Venezuela, Trinidad, and Tobago, Saint Lucia, and so on.

There are stories that a civilization existed in Ile-Ife (the citadel of Yoruba civilization) in the 8th century long before the British colonial administration. Archaeological findings in Ile-Ife prove the existence of high-level artistic skills in the 1200s to the 1400s. Artists sculpted using terra-cotta, stone, ivory, brass, bronze, and copper to create figures of traditional and cultural significance in 1300 CE. Today, after numerous political influences and division, the Yoruba ethnic group is majorly found in Ekiti, Lagos, Ogun, Ondo, Osun, Oyo, and part of Kwara, Kogi, and the Edo States in Nigeria. They can also be found in other African countries such as Egypt, Ghana, Togo, Sierra Leone, Burkina Faso, Ivory Coast, and Liberia.

Myths of creation disregarding the Big-Bang Theory

In the beginning, the universe was made up of only two elements: the sky above and the watery chaos below. Oduduwa (a servant of the Supreme Being, Olodumare) was given the task to create the Earth. He came down from heaven using a long chain, carrying a calabash filled with sand and a five-toed fowl. There wasn't a single patch of dry land, so Oduduwa poured the sand on the water and put the fowl on top of it. Everywhere the fowl stepped solid ground was formed, a chameleon was sent down to check the process and determine if the land was dry and solid enough. What remains as water today are all the places not touched by the sand. It is said that some of the objects Oduduwa brought from heaven are still in Ile-Ife, including the chain he used to climb down to earth.

This is the Yoruba mythology of the beginning of life.

They are myths that Oduduwa was a mortal who had supernatural powers, He fathered sixteen children, crowned them kings of other territories. His oldest child was named the Orangun of Ila, the Egba people of Abeokuta. Oranyan was his last-child, who ruled over the Benin Kingdom, this probably explains the striking similarity in language, food, culture, and dress between them and Yorubas. Nigeria is said to be descendants of Oduduwa's daughter named Alaketu.

Culture and Traditions

One of the most important traditions observed in the Yorubaland is "orúko àmútọ̀runwá" – the naming of a newborn child. Names are given to children by their parents, grandparents (paternal and maternal), and some other close relatives, because of this a typical Yoruba child can bear up16 different names. The circumstance surrounding a child's birth plays a significant role in the naming of the child. For example, a female child born after the death of her grandmother is called "Yetunde" which means "mother has come again".

The tradition of marriage is also a big deal for the Yoruba people, it is considered a union of not just a husband and a wife but of two families and extended families. When a young man and woman meet, they fall in love and decide to spend the rest of their lives together, then they let their parents know. The groom's parents arrange a meeting with the bride's parents for an official introduction. The agreement of the bride's dowry follows the approval of her parents.

The wedding date is set. A wedding ceremony is celebrated generously with dancing, eating, drinking, and gifts to the couple. After the celebration, "Ekun Iyawo" ritual is observed, where the bride leaves her parents and now belongs to her husband's family, she is seen crying as she is escorted by family, friends, and well-wishers to her husband's house. As part of the ritual she is prayed for and her feet are washed, to cleanse away any bad luck she might be bringing into her new home.

NIGERIA CEREMONIAL EVENTS AND THE AESTHETICS VALUE OF GELE

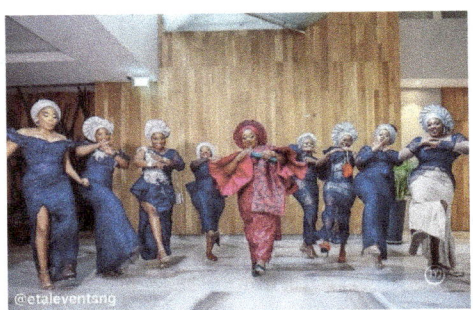

Nigerian events vary with type and significance but the main event which this book will contain are the ones with Gele as its major spice. Gele's aesthetical value in Nigeria is specific to culture and traditions practiced in some ethics groups. Gele is mostly worn by the Yorubas and Igbos for most of their ceremonial activities, e.g. Weddings, naming ceremony, introduction, Asoebi galore, Owanbe, etc.

THREE WEDDINGS

1. Introduction; Pre-Marital Introduction Ceremonies, aka "Courtship"

Courtship remains unrecognized until the formal

introduction ceremony, which means the couples are ready to tie the proverbial knot. Traditionally, the introduction ceremony happens in the family home of the bride-to-be, she dresses up in her traditional attire and flies her Gele which adds aesthetics and glamour to her look in the Yoruba and Igbo tribe. The groom-to-be comes with his family and close friends, they "pay their respects" to the bride-to-be's family and "state their intentions". After the bride-to-be's family accepts the proposal, food is served.

2. Engagement, Court Wedding/ Church Wedding

Engagement: The engagement also known as the traditional wedding is a type of ceremony which is particular to the indigenous people of the Yoruba land. The ceremony takes place mostly at the early hours of the day with the attendance of both families and as well guests. The two families (bride & groom) traditional make merry of the union of the couple. "Alaga Iduro" anchor the events thereby following a step-by-step traditional routine. During this ceremony, the bride as part of the cultural significance of the Yoruba tribe wears a beautifully wrapped gele. The bride is accompanied by her aso-ebi geles who are dressed up to accompany her through the celebration.

Court: This type of ceremony is very important as it serves as legal documentation of the union of both couples. The court wedding is a lawful form of a wedding that requires signed papers by the couple with the presence of a lawyer.

Church / Nikkai: Based on region, this ceremony differs from each other depending on individual beliefs. One is Christianity and the other is the Islamic region. If the couple is Christian, they will be joined by the pastor or reverend father. But if it's the Islamic region they will be joined together by the Alfa.

3. Reception

Nigerian brides understand it is crucial to fill out their clothes and glow on their wedding day. The extent of happiness and well-being of the bride is very much expected since her health and radiance would be assessed all through the wedding. Most importantly the reception ceremony comes last and is always the most fun. During this ceremony, the couple is allowed to have the best of their wedding highlights together dancing and having fun. Guest and family members eat and make merry of the newly wedded couples.

Some Ceremonial Celebration

Chieftaincy: The contemporary settings of the Igbo political hierarchy is held with the highest esteem, 'traditional rulers'. Traditionally kings are the head and most powerful individuals in a town who earn their position during a celebration known as chieftaincy. Chieftaincy installation ceremonies are a community-wide celebration where rulers appropriate monarchical attributes to themselves. During this chieftaincy festival, the women who hold certain powerful positions such as queens are mostly dressed a royal attire. They love to put on glamourous and beautiful costumes most especially their gele. A flamboyant gele that depicts a sense of power and royalty.

Carnivals: Carnivals are popular for their aesthetics and spectacles. They display colors and designs both in clothing, costumes, props, background designs, and as well spectacle in both music and dance. In Africa which is one of the largest continents in the world carnival celebration can be seen as one of many other celebrations. The headwrap and other head wears are famous as they are used to compliment carnival attire. Most of them are styled flamboyantly to capture the attention of on lookers.

Fashion Shows: In recent times fashion as a statement has

received lots of recognition all around the world. These have brought about fashion shows, pageants, and lots more. In the highlight of fashion shows most especially African clothing brands, headwraps are worn as a compliment to depict the culture and also to portray aesthetical values.

ASOEBI AND OWANBE

Asoebi Meaning and History

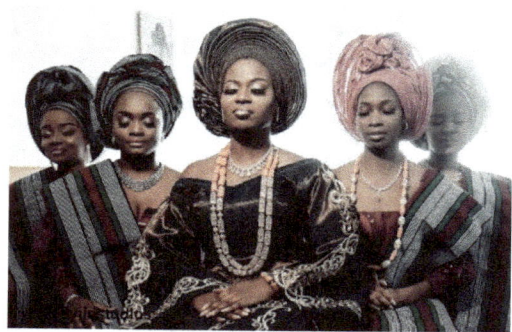

"Asoebi" are matching outfits made from identical fabric. It is a regular feature at parties, weddings, and funerals and can be seen on social media and fashion pages in Nigeria. They're called "aso" "ebi", a Yoruba phrase meaning "family cloth" and this includes gele.

It communal cultural tradition that serves as a public display of one's social relations. Majorly among the Yoruba and it is centered on family ties.

In time, distant relatives and friends are included in asoebi, birthing new and unintended forms of social anticipation and anxiety. The practice is rapidly growing in Nigeria. Though the intended functions of asoebi remain a show of love, identification, solidarity, and social bonding, due to its commodification it leads to conflict and unequal treatment of the party attendees. These vices mainly happen because some aren't financially able to buy the asoebi are left out in the distribution of souvenirs and sometimes not given food. These people experience social exclusion, embarrassment, and withdrawal from group participation. The commodification of asoebi frustrates its initial function, social bonding.

The origin of asoebi is unknown, elders over the age of 60 say originated to identify immediate family members at funerals.

A culture expert participating in our study said:

"The purpose of asoebi is to easily identify the children of the deceased during funerals, and not relatives nor friends and not for other occasions."

The established purpose of uniform dress is to inspire the idea of solidarity. When many people are communally clad, it suggests that the party host is popular and well networked. Party conveners are sometimes evaluated on the turnout of people at their events. A large crowd of attendees confers honor on the organizer among their family and friends. However, the younger generation believes it is any matching cloth chosen for an occasion.

From Funerals to Fashion

Certain traditional practices remain suitable because they reflect modification in terms of content and purpose. Asoebi experienced a major transformation during contemporary times. It extended from family members (Ebi) to co-workers (Alabasisepo), friends (ore), co-residents (Alajogbe), neighbors (Aladugbo), and other well-wishers.

In planning an event people not related by blood but connected socially can form a new kind of relationship courtesy of asoebi. Host are usually gifted in cash, material things, or in-kind (partaking in the asoebi), although cash support is highly welcomed, attendance boosts the moral and social value of the event.

A team member, also a civil servant, stated:

"The main reason that we buy and sell asoebi is to make the

event colorful, unique, and beautiful. The unique colors and styles of the asoebi wearers add value to an event."

Attending a social event is agreeing to buy the events clothe. After invitation cards have been handed out and those invited are reminded through text messages. An event with poor attendance is considered shameful and so a large group of unfamiliar are invited with the power social connection. A volunteer in our study shared:

"I have attended weddings that I did not know the couple at all or the families of the couple but I wore the same asoebi that everybody wore at the occasion. This is not the way it is supposed to be."

The Downside

Solidarity is reciprocated consciously or unconsciously especially in the asoebi community. This is in line with the Yoruba maxim, "Gbami nigba ojo, kingba e nigba erun", meaning, "One good turn deserves another".

Most times those who aren't close to the host or haven't rendered support in any form to the event, don't get special treated especially if they aren't wearing the event's asoebi. Asoebi is the basis of social segmentation at events; seating arrangement, food served, and distribution of gifts.

A team member shared her experience of not having an event's asoebi. She attended the wedding ceremony of a junior colleague who wasn't financially able to buy the wedding asoebi which cost N11,500 (US$76), sequins, and satin lace material. Though she bought a gift for her colleague and she paid the social price. She said:

"We were not allowed to enter the venue, because the seats reserved were for people of a high class, seats had name tags on them. But my colleagues defiantly occupied a table, with at least who had the asoebi on. But trays of food were passing over our heads, we aren't attended to. It took about one hour before we got anything to eat, at that point I left because I felt so bad."

MORE THAN A WRAP

Entrenching Inequality

Those who can't afford an event's asoebi and don't attend the event may avoid embarrassment and segmentation, but they lose the chance of meeting new people and networking. This form of exclusion reduces social cohesion and unity among friends. Ultimately, wealth affects relationships, participation, social integration, and power. Inequality becomes entrenched by beautiful clothing.

OWANBE MEANING AND HISTORY
(In the Spirit of Celebration)

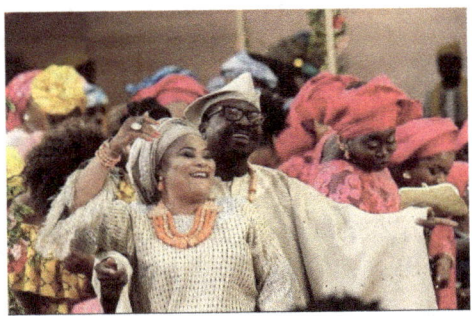

Owanbe is used to define traditional festivals that were highly anticipated in African society. Celebrations have morphed into a whole new level; they aren't yearly anymore. Now, they occur every Saturday. In Nigerian, weekends aren't complete without an Owanbe party.

Owanbe is a lavish, flamboyant party. Usually characterized by a show of luxury, color, paparazzi, food, music, dance, and networking. Parties related to Owanbe are birthdays, housewarming, naming, reunions, sometimes funerals, but mostly weddings.

Generally, the bigger the Owanbe the more it is perceived as successful.

Features of A Proper Ówàmbè

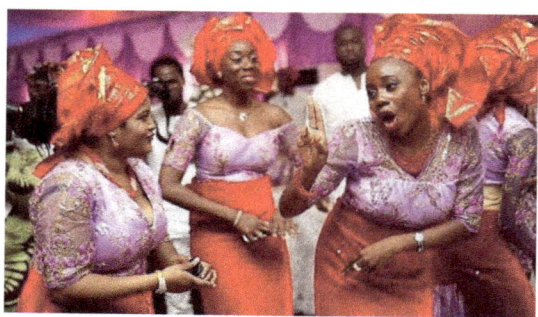

Asoebi are outfits made from matching fabric to be worn by a group for a party, wedding, or funeral. Asoebi is used for identification. For example, at a wedding, the bride's friends may wear blue and gold, the bride's family may wear white and gold, the groom's friends may wear black and pink, and so on.

Aso-Oke (traditional hand-woven material) could be cotton, damask, lace, guinea brocade, or waxed fabric (Ankara). Wearing the asoebi of an event has its benefits, several times it has been dictated the special treatment one gets at a party when he/she isn't wearing the asoebi.

1. Weekend: Parties are usually held on weekends especially Saturdays unless there is some form of crisis or lockdown.

2. Networking: Mostly, Owambes serve as family unions. Sometimes long-distance relatives meet themselves after a long time or for the first time. Asides from this, bachelors and spinsters are regulars at Owanbe, as well as the crème de la crème of the society, it is an avenue to make valuable life-defining connections.

3. Foods: The food at Owambes are always overabundant. Lucky guests get to take home the excess in organized takeaway packs, but some take as much as they can

carry. Varieties of food are served at Owambes, the most popular is Jollof rice and Amala.

Though Jollof rice is considered Legendary, it is themed a foreign food. It has given rise to an eternal battle of "who's Jollof is better, Nigeria and Ghana?"

Amala is a prominent local food especially in the western part of Nigeria, it is a solid paste food made from yam flour.

4. Mogbo-Moya: It is natural for one to attend a party him/she is not invited to. Mogbo-Moya means "I heard, so I came". Friends follow themselves to parties, while idle people could dress nice and attend a party near them. Occasionally, they don't know what the celebration is about.

5. Music, Dance, and Money-Spraying: Always expect loud music at owambes and a complimentary dance. The atmosphere is always energetic with music like Fuji, juju, and many more. Musicians who perform these local genres are prioritized, prominent musicians are King Sunny Ade, Pasuma Wonder, Saheed Osupa, Wasiu Ayinde.

Money-spraying also belongs to this mix. It is common for people to spray mint notes on the invited musician or someone dancing.

6. Souvenirs: These aren't just items given as gifts courtesy of the hosts, they're tangible evidence that one attended a party. Therefore, it is normal for people to strive to have them. Souvenirs range from handkerchiefs, buckets, hand fans, pens, bowls, and many more.

The Ówàmbè Evil Spirit

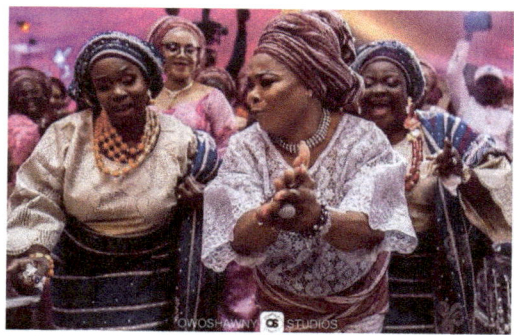

It has been observed that increasingly ladies remain unmarried because their finance isn't financially able to afford the wedding of their dreams. Wedding gowns are now more expansive than previously planned and yet it was only worn once in a lifetime.

There are cases where parents forgo important things like their children's educational welfare, to organize or be part of Owambe. Low-income earners subscribe to thrift associations for the benefit of funding Owambe activities. Many feel it has descended into what Federick Nwabufo described as a "fast eroding culture of money management, prudence, modesty, chivalry, discipline and spiritual values in Nigeria".

The Prominent Gains

The atmosphere of an Owanbe can't be ignored; the color, the glamour, the merriment, and the excitement, are experiences people always look forward to. Owanbe is one of few areas that strengthen the communal spirit of Nigerians, having risen to be one of the most unifying factors in the African society; bringing people from different tribes to one venue to share happiness, wear similar clothes, and eat from the same pot.

Owambe is an indicator where Africans can overlook ethnic boundaries and stand in unity to celebrate success. One of the glamorous features of owanbe is the complementary aesthetics, Gele. It was impossible to have an Owanbe party without Gele as the central attraction. Many Nigerian women attend Owanbe to show off their beautifully crafted Gele.

Growing up, my mother sometimes won't go to a party until she gets her Gele properly and glamorously, which made me wonder if the main purpose of going to the event was to showcase her Gele. Geles due to their irresistible beauty and aesthetical value is now one of the most popular and anticipated recipes in African society (event), especially in Nigeria.

CHAPTER 3
TYPES OF GELE AND THE ROLES THEY PLAY

Gele, popular and iconic complimentary attire in Africa particularly Nigeria comes in various fascinating styles. As art, it is a creativity of a stylist who has mastered it and begun to evolve it by creating unique and outstanding styles.

Today, geles are revamped and celebrated in Nigerian traditional culture; an explosion of creativity, combined with innate cultural pride. Meaning women treat the geles not just as an accessory but sometimes as the main focus of their attire. Gele now comes with scalloped edges, laser-cut designs, beaded (by hand), two-tone effects, Swarovski-encrusted, hand-painted, embroidered, sequined, and any design you can imagine.

The Gele is a traditional Nigerian Headwrap, majorly worn for special occasions as an accessory complementing the traditional "iro" (a wrap skirt) and "buba" (a loose-fitting blouse). Gele is usually made out of heavy or stiff fabric that can be wrapped and molded into a specific shape. Fabrics from Switzerland and Austria are popular, but the Yoruba "aso oke" is indigenous and the general preference.

Originally, Aso Oke is a ceremonial fabric woven locally, made up of strands of cotton and/or silk. Aso Oke is generally used to make Iro and Buba for very special occasions like the bride's wedding dress. In 1960, geles were tied to mimic the architecture of Nigeria's first skyscraper. When the National Theatre was built with a peaked roof to mimic a general's cap, Nigerian fashionistas folded and twisted their geles to echo the design.

From the rolling together in folds to the forming of uneven pleats gele has become a professional and complex art that needs to be learned and is now a service provided by professional headgear stylists and by most makeup artists and salons, in Nigeria and Nigerian communities across the world. Today's towering and intricate styles are best executed with a thin, crisp rectangle of cloth imported from Switzerland. Its paperlike consistency is ideal for folding, wrapping, and layering. There are many ways to tie a gele. Tying isn't the only option as some gele experts will create the style on a base and stitch it down, so you put it on like a hat.

Types of Gele Materials

Asooke: Asooke is a popular fabric in Nigeria which is mostly associated with wedding ceremonies. This material is made with cotton and it is being weaved by a professional manually. In recent times asooke has evolved into different designs and patterns. E.g grantex, supernet, jawu, and lots more. With gele being diverse the casual ones are usually made from the same fabric as the outfit being worn. It could also be a regular polyester scarf or shawl that is worn as a head-tie.

Sego: These are Gele made for the fashion-conscious and the fashionista of the Nigerian and other African cultures. In this category, we have Grand Swiss, Super Jubilee, and Hayes Gele. Also, we have the "Net Gele Head" tie (a net-like, see-through fabric gele), these are imported gele made with the African woman and culture in mind. They are made in Switzerland and come in solid colors, with designs and embroideries.

Embellished or Bling Gele: Accessorizing Gele

As mentioned earlier, the common way of accessorizing with Gele is wearing traditional outfits, Buba and the Iro (Yoruba style) or George (Igbo style). Contemporarily, modern Nigerian women have found new ways to accessorize Geles. The latest trend is to bling up the geles. This is called Bling

MORE THAN A WRAP

Gele.

Bling Gele is becoming popular among fashionistas who take Gele wearing to another level. To bling is adding precious stones, beads, rhinestones, and sometimes silk flowers to the Gele for a more glamorous appeal. Blink Geles set one apart, like the celebrant of an occasion; wedding, wedding anniversary, or a milestone birthday celebration.

GELE STYLES

The popular styles in Nigeria are;

1.

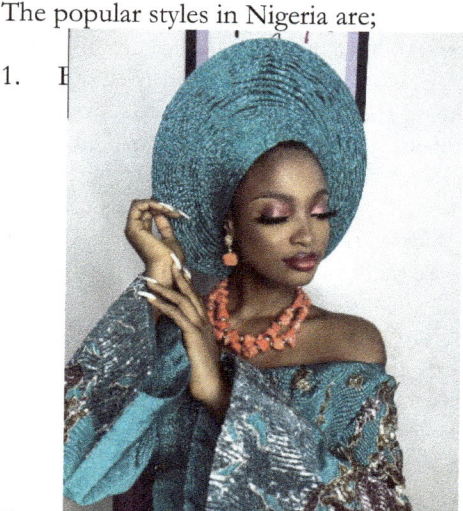

2. Bridal fan Gele

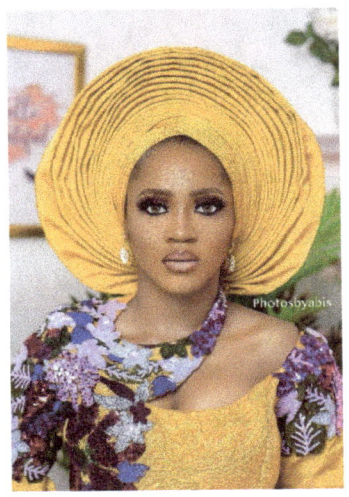

3. Fan Gele

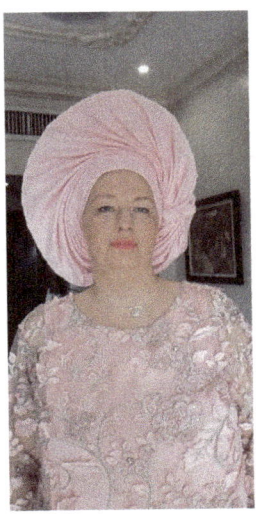

The above styles are the top styles, which birthed different and unique variations. These styles are invented by professional headgear stylists in Nigeria and Africa at large. In creating styles of headgear, the power of imagination inspires art.

Other Styles Are;

- Avant-Garde Gele
- Twisted Fan Gele
- Half twisted Fan Gele
- Zigzag Gele
- Bow Tie Gele
- Ruffles Pleat Gele
- Unconventional Styles
- Double Gele

GELE STYLIST IN NIGERIA

In Nigeria today, headwrap stylist numbers are on the rise some of which are:

- EnnyGeleCraft
- Onigele
- T-boy Gele
- Segun Gele
- Ighogele
- Sagsignature
- Geleloge
- Taiwo's Touch and many more

Each stylist has a significant contribution to the growth of Africa Headgear Craft (Gele).

A prominent African Gele stylist is Segun Gele, he is a Nigerian, a make-up artist, and an entrepreneur based in the United States. His works were featured on CNN for his flamboyant gele style, a fashion attire of significant importance to West African women's fashion culture.

Another prominent African Gele stylist is Tolulope Adedara, a Nigeria-based Gele stylist who has inspired and empowered many Gele stylists in Nigeria. He is also the founder of Onigele, Onigele is a headgear company with great visions and is taking the gele craft to the next level.

Thirdly, Fatola Eniola Evans, CEO EnnyGeleCraft and author of this book. Fatola Eniola is a Nigerian-based Gele stylist who has inspired and created empowerment opportunities through skill acquisition for both employed and unemployed Nigerians through physical and virtual tutoring.

ROLES OF GELE IN AN AFRICAN CONTEXT

A beautiful Headwrap "Gele" is sure to make one stand out in the crowd of any occasion. A bride-to-be will desire a trendy gele style for her traditional wedding attire. A bride is meant to look exceptional simply because she is the center of attention and she always wants to wear the latest and a beautifully wrapped gele.

When shopping for traditional attire it's important to ensure the texture of the gele fabric is of good quality and would best suit your attire. Other traditional roles of gele were pointed out in chapter one, history of head wrap in Africa

CHAPTER 4

THE SOCIO-CULTURAL IMPORTANCE OF GELE IN AFRICA

ASOEBI, A CASE STUDY

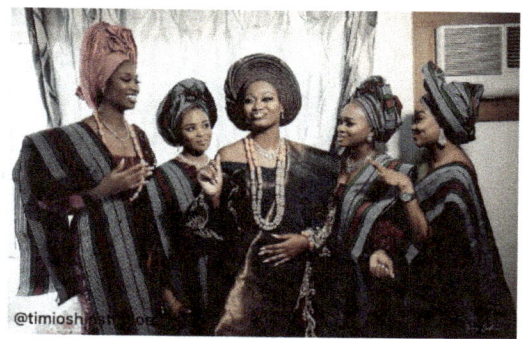

In recent years, research and theory on socio-economic development have given rise to two contending schools of thought. One emphasizes the convergence of values as a result of "modernization". This thought process is said to predict the declination of traditional values and their replacement with "modern" values by rationality, tolerance, trust, and participation.

The other thought process emphasizes the persistence of traditional values despite the economic and political changes. This thought process believes that values are independent of economic conditions, this implies that the evolution of some set of modern values is unlikely and traditional values will continue to exert their independent influence on the cultural changes caused by economic development.

One of the cultural traditions that have endured despite

modernization in Nigeria is the Yoruba tribe Asoebi practice and inclusion of Gele. Asoebi being originally a uniform dress worn by family members in social events is now a practice that includes a network of unfamiliarity and transcended the Yoruba ethnic group now gradually becoming a national culture.

This practice is currently enjoying appreciable transformations in terms of its contents and it is dynamic cultural natural. Pelto 1966, writing on cultural dynamism states:

"Each new generation reshuffles and changes the systems of ideas, meanings and rules so that the social tradition is never fixed and unchanging in any society".

From the above statement, a hasty look at the Nigerian contemporary social milieu reveals that while some cultural practices are declining and some even going into extinction n, there are yet others that are experiencing increased acceptance and popularity with some level of modifications. These transformations, modifications, or actual rejection of some practices are predicated upon both external and internal exigencies.

Clothing is a curial part of everyday life. Through clothes, individuals establish a sense of self and social status. Despite the much literature on dressing across the scientific, popular board, and high profile international conferences on themes that range from clothing and imperialism to fashion and consumption show of dress scholarship.

Clothing is classified under "fashion" in sociological literature and is dealt has as an ongoing scene of competition and struggle, as ostentatious consumption, which primarily indicates the social status of those buying, owning, and dressing in a specific garment, (Bohn 2004).

Fashion in Sombart's (1902) theory of modern demand creation is an excellent example of luxurious consumption. Barber and Lobel (1953), give a rehabilitating account of American middle-class women's fashion habits, calling it quite rational if interpreted as a representation of status considered in its latent functionality for the reproduction of the American social structure. For Bourdieu (1975, 1980), fashion designers and their various brands are symbols of distinction in the magic of the social field of fashion wherein a manifold struggle, primary positions, the definition of the rules of the game, and the legitimate construction of reality are fought out, (cited in Bohn 2004).

The concept of asoebi and gele is reported broadly in the popular press and the internet blogosphere, there is little scholarly research on the topic. With the use of archival records, books, journals, interviews, observation, and oral tradition, this book tests the position that socioeconomic development is related to major cultural changes and the persistence of distinctive cultural traditions. It questions the dialectics of stability and dynamism of culture in a rapidly changing world. Specifically, this book examines the origin of asoebi and gele, its sociological relevance, and trends in the growth of the art, which necessitated its transformation from an ethnic-cultural attire into a national culture among Nigerians both home and beyond. To achieve these objectives, this book is conceptualized in two broad analytical frameworks – cultural commodification and factionalism.

ORIGINS OF ASO-EBI

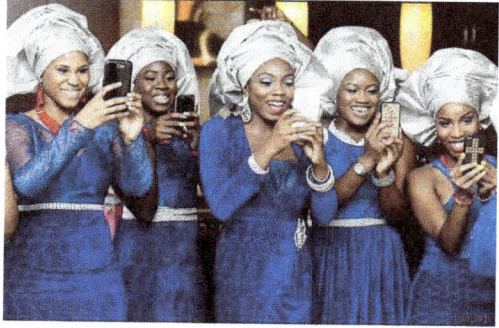

MORE THAN A WRAP

In Yoruba, "Aso" means cloth while "Ebi" means family, therefore means family clothes. The Yoruba tribe holds fashion in high esteem. Having good fashion sense played a significant role in the Yoruba class system; the importance is attached to the size, color, quality, and quantity of the fabric. Modes of dressing in Yoruba "traditional" society followed a hierarchical order which often established seniority with prestige and expensive outfits. Social anthropological photographic evidence from decades-old suggest the native Yoruba woven fabrics known as "Aso Oke" were the natural choice of asoebi before the advent of imported fabrics. Apparently, due to the poor mechanization of these native fabrics and the inability to meet the demand, particularly from the period of Nigerian independence the gradual rise in demand got answered by imported fabrics like lace. However, the embroideries such brands as sanyan and alaari in the aso oke family had, imported lace fabrics are near equal.

There are two theories related to the origin of Asoebi in the Yoruba tribe. The first theory, views asoebi as an ancient phenomenon, while the second links asoebi emergence with unmatched growth that came with the post-war I boom of 1918-20. Though Olukoju believes asoebi was part of a culture of "conspicuous consumption that was fuelled by the post-World War I boom, which has survived to this day as a national culture", (cited in Nwafor 2011).

William Bascom traced the origins of asoebi to Yoruba demography that used the uniformed dressing or used as a mark fraternal bonds. He observed men and women clubs were characterized by their uniform clothing, which members could be recognized during religious or other ceremonies (ibid).

For Marjorie Keniston Mcintosh, the use of "same fabric or color of clothing, the same style of dress, or at least a similar head tie demonstrates the size and standing of women in their associations known as egbe" (ibid).

Asoebi started as a family funeral activity or rites, those required to wear asoebi were children and siblings of the deceased. John and Margaret Drewal categorized uniform dressing as a form of comradeship whose origin is in the pairing of Yoruba Gelede masquerades. They wrote: "when two partners make a pact and adopt a common secret name, they often choose to dress alike and may be mistaken for twins".

Whichever of these theories you adopt note that asoebi has continued to attract attention, it is a dress culture in Nigeria for social ceremonies be it weddings, naming ceremonies, birthdays, burial ceremonies, political gatherings, house warming parties, and so on.

There are three major reasons why asoebi has continued to find social acceptance in contemporary Nigerian society.

- First, many Nigerian communities enjoy a thriving cultural social life. Though many communities are informal and semi-formal organizations, many people love these social activities, which often substitute for the missing formal or state institutions that tend to persist during periods of repression, negligence, or co-optation. This form of social life provides a good platform for the growth and promotion of this age-long dress practice.
- Second, there is a need for one to construct their meaning of self, social identity and social relations has gone a long way in the adoption and growth of asoebi over time among all tribes in Nigeria.

In addition, a thriving urban life provides a fertile ground for the survival of this form of ostentatious consumption.

SOCIOLOGY OF ASOEBI

Beyond the glamour and fun attached to uniformed dressing, asoebi is first and foremost a form of identification with communal ethos, with the collective. According to Familusi (2010):

"a distinguished feature of Africaness in the spirit of oneness manifesting in "we feeling", live and let live, serious concern for others and fraternity. This is born out of unavoidable interaction with other members of society. In other words, no man is an island."

In Nigerians especially the Yorubas, asoebi reinforces social identity and solidarity among group members. Social identification is a system we use to define ourselves in terms and categories, picking out what we have in common with people. In contrast to personal identity characterizations, which may be highly idiosyncratic, social identities assume commonalities with others.

The term "Identity" is widely used and consequential can mean different things to different people. Identity is sometimes used to refer to a sense of integration of the self, in which different aspects come together in a unified whole. However, "social identity" refers to those aspects of a person that are defined in terms of his or her group memberships. Although most people are members of many groups, some of those groups are meaningful in terms of how we define ourselves.

In these cases, self-definition is shared with other people who also claim that categorical membership, for example, Anita is a woman, a Muslim, a marathon runner, and a member of PDP. Sharing a similar social identity with others doesn't mean one interacts with every member of that category. It does mean we share numerous features with other members of different category and to some degree, events that are relevant to the group have a certain significance for the individual member.

Many social identities exist, reflecting many ways in which people connect to other groups and social categories. These include ethnic and religious identities, political identities, vocations and avocations, personal relationships, and stigmatized groups. Each of these types of social identification has some unique characteristics that make it somewhat different from another type, (Deaux 2001).

Asoebi is (and continues) to serve as a means of identification, as the wearers at social events are implicitly demonstrating that they are proud to be identified with the celebrant, (Familusi 2010).

Celebrants choose fabrics of their, for friends, colleagues or well-wishers is being identified, (ibid).

In many instances, the adornment of asoebi attracts special recognition. The need to construct their meaning of self, social identity, and social relations has fuelled the growth of asoebi over time among the Yoruba and in Nigeria as a whole.

Family to the issue of social identity is the principle of reciprocity. An individual who buys asoebi to celebrate an occasion expects others to buy when his or her celebration comes. Buying and wearing asoebi at social events is an indication of support from the group member and thus ensures the group's survival and stability.

In Nigerian traditional society, the principle of reciprocity operates in both social and economic transactions. According to Dopamu and Alana (2004):

"Co-operation and mutual helpfulness are virtues among the Yoruba. There is a limitation to what a single individual can achieve all alone. The co-operation of others is highly important in achieving most goals. It is believed that when two hands join in washing each other, one will have a truly clean hand... It is also taught that while it is easy to break a broomstick, it is not easy to break a full bunch of them."

Equally evident is the trans-class dimension of asoebi. This practice has transcended class barriers; the rich and poor can access the democratic agency of asoebi. It is a practice that accommodates all. Some claim that asoebi eliminates hitherto existing class differences as nearly everyone wearing asoebi on an occasion is identified as the same regardless of social status. Albeit temporarily, it gives the poor a sense of fulfillment and relief from a feeling of financial inadequacy, (Sofola in Familusi

2010).

Though this role of social leveler has been defeated because there can be as many as five asoebi at a single party. Some wear the not-so-expensive Ankara fabrics, some may be gorgeously dressed in an expensive asoebi, therefore creating segmentation between the rich and the poor.

Cultural Commodification

"Commodification" is used in describing the process by which something that does not have an economic value is assigned a value and hence how market values can replace other social values. It defines modification of relationships, formerly untainted by commerce, into commercial relationships in everyday use.

"Cultural Commodification" is considered packaging culture for sale; establishing a value, in terms of labor or real monetary value. This transformation occurred in the asoebi dress practice.

Crook, Pakulski, and Waters (1992), identified three main characteristics of modern culture, named: differentiation, rationalization, and commodification. According to them, the commodification of culture is turning cultural values into products, commodities that can be readily sold and bought.

With the increasing participants of asoebi, the practice is more than uniform, it is fast becoming a form of economic transaction. The cost of asoebi depends on the caliber of people involved, some choose affordable materials others go for high-class and expensive fabrics.

There are asoebi purchased by the social class, the high class may cost approximately ₦150,000 and above, the middle class may cost between ₦13000 and ₦15,000, lower-class are comfortable between ₦1500 to ₦5000.

According to Crook et al, taste develops when people have enough resources to make some choices about what they consume. In early modernity, only the highest classes could do this, but progressing happened the possibility of choosing what to consume spread to all classes. This does not undermine the hierarchies of taste, the taste of higher social classes is still valued above that of lower classes.

Allude to the above statement is, the development of taste is a key feature of modern culture.

"Mass culture is imposed from above. It is fabricated by technicians, hired by businessmen; its audiences, and passive consumers, their participation limited to the choice between buying or not buying. The Lords of kitch, in short, exploit the cultural needs of the masses to make a profit and /or to maintain their class rule", (Macdonald 1957).

The term "Popular Culture" is often used in similar ways as the term "Mass Culture". Popular culture is any cultural value appreciated by a large number of ordinary people with little pretensions to its cultural expertise. However, mass culture is used as a pejorative term, a contrast to popular culture.

Crook et al claim that contemporary societies are moving towards post-modernity. Complementing this, we adapt two of Dominic Strinati 1995's five main features of post-modern analysis of popular culture.

The first feature of postmodernism is the "breakdown of the distinction between culture and society", this involves the development of a "media-saturated society". In such a society, mass media is extremely powerful, the media becomes consumed and creates a false sense of reality instead of reflecting reality. The mass media, television, and fashion magazines have continued to define the Nigerian fashion trend. Computer technology creates virtual realities which "potentially replace their real-life counterparts". Increasingly, economic activity is concerned with buying and selling media images rather than physical products.

The second feature of postmodernism is "an emphasis on style at the expense of substance". This particular cultural value becomes popular because they have designer labels that evoke an attractive lifestyle, rather than because they are useful. Society develops a "designer ideology". Surface qualities assume more importance than anything deeper.

Global economic capitalism promotes profit-making above any other considerations. The major promoters of asoebi are merchants and celebrants. Cloth vendors love making sales, the celebrants use part of the proceeds to procure gifts and special entertainment for the buyers. Other in the economic transactions are printers who emboss on souvenir items, photographers, tailors, and owners of fashion magazine outfits.

ASOEBI AND FASHIONISM

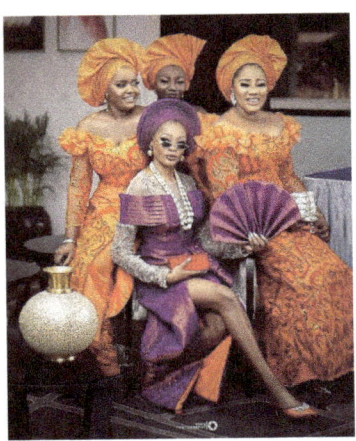

The word factionalism was coined by combining "fashion" and "nationalism". Fashionism is closely linked to popular culture, it is a popular culture trend blending patriotism with fashion. It is usually used to mark the emergence of local brands' popularity. The term is attributed to Italian educated

Filipino fashion designer, Rhett Eala, who created a collection of collared shirts and Polos for the brand Collezione C2 in 2006, strategically using the Philippine archipelago for its main design.

One issue that has come to prominence in the understanding of transnational relations is the identification of the human body as an important contact zone where the foreign and the domestic meet, and where national identities emerge in direct response to and in collaboration with transnational influences.

Asoebi crossed the cultural boundaries of the Yoruba tribe decades ago and was mainstreamed as one of the key elements of Nigeria's national culture. In the past five decades, asoebi and its associated cultural practices have passed the borders of Nigeria, it has spread to other parts of West Africa, taking on local inflections and adaptations from Ghana to Liberia, Gambia to Zambia, and spreading to the diaspora.

Hence, the ability of asoebi to transgress ethnic boundaries and be practiced among the Igbo, Hausa, and other ethnic groups in Nigeria is a sign of unification through dress at a national level.

Nowadays, asoebi is seen more like a Nigerian culture than as a Yoruba cultural phenomenon, (Nwafor 2012). This harmonization is seen also in the spelling and written derivatives of the word used by the Igbo who pronounce and spell it as ashebi. Asoebi also popular in northern Nigeria is called Yaye (vogue) or Anko. These are indicative of the fact that the practice is a borrowed culture from the Yoruba tribe.

In Nigeria today, apart from football, asoebi has played a significant role in the constitution of an image belonging to Nigeria. The practice has promoted "traditional dress" culture in opposition to the influence of "Western dress" culture, seen in the rejection of European suits and style of garments for most public outings in Nigeria.

Conclusion

In this chapter, cultural commodification and factionalism are treated as adaptive responses to global economic capitalism. Originally, asoebi was meant to be a family uniform, among the Yoruba tribe of Nigeria, this was done for the guests to identify members of the family during the occasion. But now, it is a medium of economic transaction and has diffused into Nigeria as a whole.

Asoebi practice is now a trend that has taken over the Nigerian fashion scene, dresses are made from Aso oke, Java, Ankara, Silk, George, and guinea materials. With the continued expansion of the global cash nexus economy and the need to create a distinct Nigerian identity, the asoebi dress practice will no doubt continue to be relevant in a fast-changing world.

The Headwrap or Headgear, Gele, plays a very vital role in an African society which are;

- It promotes and adds beauty to the cultural values and traditions of Africans.
- It adds glamour to an event or celebration
- It is African art.
- It is one of the major highlights in most events
- It tells a story about a person"s personality
- It is a form of fashion
- It adds beauty to a woman.

CHAPTER 5

AFRICAN GELE IN OTHER PARTS OF THE WORLD: A PROGNOSIS

The further away our black history goes, the more important it is for us to be informed about it. Today's youth don't know the struggles their grandparents faced. There's much to learn, much to understand and this chapter hopes to educate you about the deep-rooted history and rich heritage we have.

Headwrap during Slavery

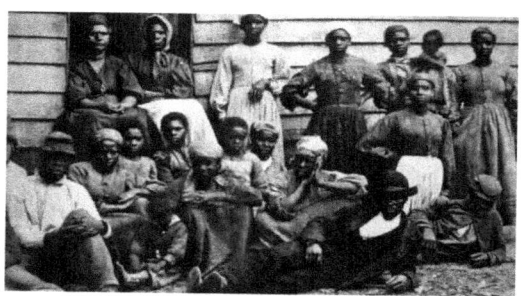

Before the American Revolution happened, a growing concern arose amongst slave masters. Wives of the slave masters were getting attracted to the unique skin tones, hair textures, and varying "shades of brown". This is not surprising, though many cultures, then and now, think lighter skin is more beautiful, history says black is beautiful.

Due to slave masters' wives' complaints, the European colonies created laws to oppress this attraction. In 1735, South

Carolina passed the Negro Act, a law that listed the types of clothing blacks were allowed to wear. On that list was a section that stated women must wear their hair bound in a kerchief, which was the start of the humble Headwrap.

This handkerchief was to mark the inferior status of blacks but it also had its perks. Female Slaves were sent to work all day in the fields and this headwrap protected them from the blazing sun, as well as from lice and perspiration.

This was not enough to keep the workers down. In some parts of Central America, women there got creative. As stated in chapter one, women found ways to fold their Headwraps to communicate with each other oblivious to their slavers.

In 1785, the Spanish colonial governor, Esteban Rodriguez Miró, demanded afro-creole women to wear tignons (a turban-like Headwrap). It was an attempt to hinder their exotic allure, this failed as the women rebelled by decorating their wraps with amazing colors, ribbons, feathers, and jewels. These beautiful head-wrap displays evoked a sense of freedom and became a bold fashion statement.

HEADWRAP IN AMERICA

Headwraps migrated to America in the 1700s. African American Headwrap is often associated with stereotypes and was used as a means of oppression. The Negro Act of 1735 was one of the first forms of oppression that forced African Americans to wear certain clothing to identify slaves from free blacks.

The difference between the African Headdress and the African American Headdress is the shift in the symbolism behind the clothing and the wearers of the clothing. The Headdress served as protection from the sun, covered their hair when it was not presentable, protected them from lice infestation, and identified the woman as a slave.

The functionality of headwraps in the U.S. derived

from the need for slaves to keep hair out of their faces and protect themselves against the heat. However, its social role was to stop exoticism and tempt men from sexually abusing slave women, but that didn't work. Though the headdress marked women as slaves they became a means of empowerment. The headwrap became uniquely their own, and they learned how to distinguish themselves through different tying styles.

Fast forward 200 years and black American singers, actresses, and activists continued wearing headwraps as both a racial symbol and cultural unity. Culturally, headwraps are not exclusive to black or African women, but because of their historical significance in a country known for racial tension, it has raised some debate.

The black hair fashion has stood the test of time and space, despite the dispersal of African communities due to the Trans-Atlantic slave trade, the Great Migration, and globalization.

The headwrap links black women of the West with the traditions of their ancestors, and with their cousins across the Atlantic.

Throughout the antebellum American South, South America, and the Caribbean, many slave masters required enslaved black women to wear head coverings. Though headwraps were symbolic markers, an indicator of slave inferiority in the social hierarchy, enslaved black women found many creative ways to resist, like, in Suriname, black women used the folds in their headscarves to communicate coded messages to one another.

In Afro-creole culture, despite oppression in 18th century Louisiana, free mixed-race creole community's headwraps served as a buffer class between powerful whites and enslaved blacks. French and Spanish men sought and forced relationships with women of color. This made the race and class lines increasingly obscure.

In 1785, Spanish colonial governor Esteban Rodriguez Miró mandated that Afro-Creole women wear a turban-like head-wrap, tignons, to undermine their "exotic" attraction but became a defiant fashion statement for free women of color.

In 1865, after the United States abolished slavery, some black American women continued creatively to wear headwraps. The style became associated with servitude and homeliness. The mass production of mammy images like "Aunt Jemima" wearing a checker hair tie reinforced such stigmas.

Many black women began embracing Eurocentric standards of beauty and professionalism. Resulting, wearing headscarves in public a fall out in black communities during the early 20th century. However, women continued to wrap their hair in silk or satin scarves at home to preserve pressed hairstyles throughout the week.

During the 1970s, headwraps became a central accessory of the Black Power uniform of rebellion. The head-wrap, like the Afro, embraced a style once used to shame people of African descent. "Black is beautiful", kente head-wraps were Afrocentric aesthetic celebration.

In the antebellum South, enslaved black women were forced to wear kerchiefs or headwraps as part of their uniforms. Fears rose over the consequences of violent white male lust and potential Negro rebellion. From plantation owners to politicians, individual and collective black expressions were seen as impending upheaval.

Regulating the dress code of the black population made the white society feel in control and exercise the right to clamp down on any perceived civil disobedience or law-breaking.

The head-wrap (as discussed in chapter one) became in an image that depicted black women as "mammies", catering to the needs of their masters and mistresses. Songs like "Aunt Jemima", written and performed by comedian Billy Kersands in 1875, and products like the Pearl Milling Company's "Aunt Jemima's Pancake Flour" mix popularized the image of black women as sassy but motherly figures whose purpose was to coddle the Whites.

But efforts to tie the dress code of African descendants to their inferior status under white supremacy created an environment where slaves adopted innovative ways to express themselves under the tyranny of their masters but were evolved into a proud identity marker. Tanisha C. Ford, professor of black studies and history, in an interview said, "The head-wrap quickly became a way for black women to reclaim their sense of humanity".

In early 2000, the first chemical relaxers were introduced. Annie Malone's "Great Wonderful Hair Grower" and the more successful C.J. Walker's "Wonderful Hair Grower", allowed black women to chemically straighten their hair. This promised instant hair growth upon application. Activists like Booker T. Washington criticized these relaxers for encouraging the internalization of European beauty standards. But the headwrap became more functional; headwraps protected the hair from sweat, water, and dust, which would interfere with the effectiveness of the hair grower.

HISTORY OF DURAG HEADWRAP

What Is a Durag

MORE THAN A WRAP

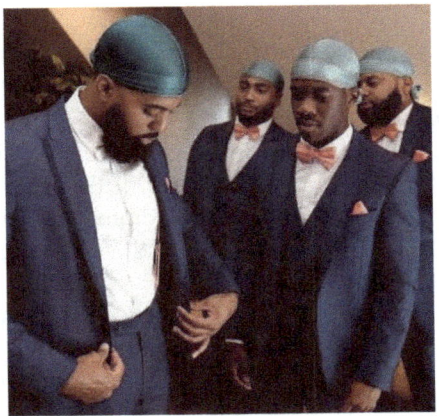

Durag is a piece of cloth or a wave cap that is worn around the head. It is said to accelerate waves' development, dreadlocks, and braids. They are also used to keep the wave patterns at the place while sleeping. It is mostly made of silk, velvet, and various types of fabrics. An iteration of the head-wrap is "Durag", a pressing cap used to protect chemically treated hair from sweat, water, and dust.

Durag Origin

During the 1900s, durag was worn by black slaves to hold their hair and used to maintain hairstyles, during the Harlem Renaissance in the 1930s. Late in the 1960s, men started wearing it, this was after the Black Power Movement, and durag became the leading fashion statement, and various athletes, wrappers, and so on. Durag lost its popularity in the 2000s but due to rappers like A$AP Ferg, Meek Mill, and other celebrities, the popularity of waves arose so as durags. Nowadays, it's worn by many celebrities of both genders as a fashion statement. They come in different colors and fabrics, and use by people of all ages of both genders.

MORE THAN A WRAP

Who Created Them?

There is no history on the creator of durag can be traced back to the 70s. However, Darren Dowdy, the president of "So Many Waves", claims his dad, William J. Dowdy, invented Durag as a crucial part of the hair grooming kit. He called durag a tie-down and was first sold in 1979. Darren Dowdy further added that his father wanted to keep the hair in place, and the idea was to keep a natural, tightly coiled hair structure in place, tie-down is used to protect hair patterns.

Why Was It Created

Thanks to the way our hair grows out, but keeping them down and free from frizzing could be challenging. To keep 360 waves at the place, hair must lay down and stay down, and that's why durag was invented. These can sit tight on the head, and help make the hair flat. Similarly, braids can have the same issue that 360 waves do, frizzy over time. Durags were invented to work for keeping braids together, especially while sleeping.

Originally, in the 19th century, durag was worn to label poor African-American laborers and slaves. However, it was in the 1930s, during the era of the "Great Depression" and "Harlem Renaissance" the usage of the durag started to change. Popular hairstyle waves were born and Durags preserve this hairstyle. Hairstyles like Waves, which are curly or combed down and flattened in ripple patterns simulating that of sea waves.

Ethnic Dress in the United States: A Cultural Encyclopaedia cites the 1930s as the first period in which the durag was used, increasingly by black men, to maintain hairstyles such as the conk, which manipulated the hair into soft waves. The conk was spotted by jazz musicians like Duke Ellington and Cab Calloway.

The rise of the Black Power movement during the late 1960s and '70s bought about the decline of chemically processed hair. Headwraps, durag, remained cultural staples in American fashion more so with the rise of hip-hop in the 1980s.

Durag, a simple cloth meant to reinforce the lowly status of Black Americans is now a powerful expression of identity.

HISTORY OF TURBAN HEADWRAP

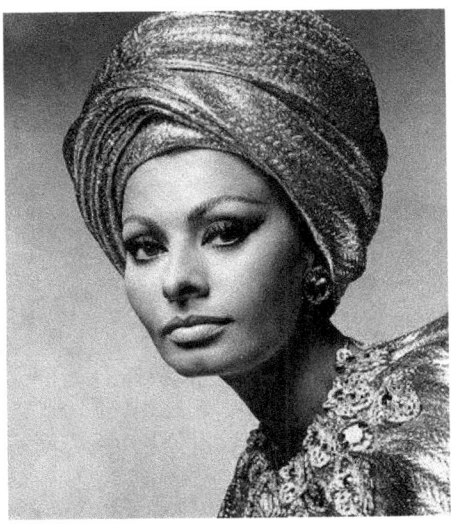

Turbans are headgears, fabrics of different widths and lengths, which are twisted and turned around the head. The wrapped folds are derived to produce a "fitted effect" akin to a stitched or an engineered head covering, though length, style, color, and fabric may vary, the basic concept and construction of turban remain.

With many forms existing this is probably the widest and most flexible definition of durag. It is popular in rural areas in Persia, the Middle East, Turkey, parts of Africa, and the Indian subcontinent where wrapped, as opposed to stitched headgear, continues to be preferred.

Origin

Little is known of the origins of the turban, but the earliest evidence, dating from 2350 BCE, of a turban-like garment is from Mesopotamia in a royal sculpture. Therefore, the origin of the turban cannot be ascribed to religion alone, since was in use before the advent of Islam and Christianity. Also, it is mentioned in the Old Testament and Vedic literature from India. A sculpture from Central India dated100 BCE provides detailed visual evidence of turbans.

The headdress was originally worn by royalty and spiritual leaders, used to commute power, is often being adorned with accessories and jewels to display wealth and grandeur.

The first documentation of turban as a fashion accessory was in 1665, in an iconic Dutch painting, "Girl with a Pearl Earring", by Johannes Vermeer. The oil painting was of a European girl wearing an exotic dress, a large pearl earring, and a turban tied around her head. Said to be inspired by Turkish traditions of that time. In 2003, this painting was made into a film starring Scarlett Johansson and Colin Firth, which revived the styles of wearing this particular type of turban.

In the 1800 and 1900, turban fashion popularity grew, its draped variety dominated the fashion scene. Comfortable and without religious connotations, turbans became increasingly popular with women.

The Regency era – a fashion said to be inspired by the increased trade with India, took hold of the turban style, making it a statement of class and wealth. These days the style of the turban was initially simple, but as its popularity grew and hairstyles became more elaborate so did the styles of turban, as it was often being decorated with jewels and worn to evening balls and functions.

Fast forward to the 20th century, turbans were revived as a fashion accessory once again! Fashion designer Paul

Poiret, also known as "Sultan de la mode" was said to have revived the "oriental" turban during the early 1910s. Being a fan of the Victoria and Albert Museum, he regularly paid a visit to admire its collection of antique turbans, where he got inspired to revive the fashion statement once again.

With the introduction of cars and motorcycles in the 1920s, it wasn't hard for turbans to gain popularity again, thanks to their functionality to control a woman's hair when traveling in a vehicle. Turbans were often made of silk or velvet and adorned with feathers or brooches.

During the war turbans remained popular, it was functional and served a purpose shampoo and hair products were rationed and their design was of that that could be created with minimal sewing skills and time. After the war, the turban made it to Hollywood. With actresses like Greta Garbo, and Gloria Swanson wearing turbans designed by French milliner, Madame Paulette.

Leaping to the 1950s, the draped turban had yet another revival. In 1955, Christian Dior designed a turban that was worn by Elizabeth Parke Firestone. The socialite was known for her bold fashion choices, and reports of her wearing a grey wool turban many times between 1955 and 1960 were made. German actress Marlene Dietrich was also known to have worn turban designed by Christian Dior. As hairstyles changed, turban styles were adapted to cover the bouffant hair trend of the fifties and sixties. Milliner Claude Saint-Cyr, who designed hats for HRH, The Queen, in 1956 created a soft textured turban that covered the ears and rose to a draped peak at the back of the head. Turbans became one of Her Majesty's signature hats in the 60s and 70s. In 1979 she wore a blue layered turban on a visit to the Gulf region, and on a trip to Mexico, she wore a bright yellow polka dot variation.

Yet again, Turbans had a popularity boost in the 1970s, with Biba fashion house leading the way in quirky styles. Biba designed feathered turbans that were worn by the likes of Twiggy and Jean Shrimpton. The turbans were worn with kaftans or loose silk blouses, a look that became popular in the

'20s. Actresses including Elizabeth Taylor and Joan Collins began wearing turbans as day and evening wear. After the revival of turbans in the '70, turbans took a back seat throughout the '18s and '19s due to their edgy styles.

In 2007, Prada displayed turbans as part of their spring/summer collection. And in 2010, we see Sarah Jessica Parker making the accessories noticeably popular again in "Sex and the City 2". She wore a gold silk turban from Ralph Lauren's 2009 spring collection, the actress was also seen wearing one off-screen when she attended the premiere of the movie. Other fashion houses picked up from Ralph Lauren and Prada, started creating turbans routinely for the catwalk, with Jason Wu, and Giorgio Armani displaying turbans in their following collections. Milliner Philip Treacy joined in.

In 2018, the turban was seen as holiday wear, with a relaxed feel to them turbans were worn with kaftans and swimsuits for vacation, as demonstrated by Emilio Pucci for its spring/summer '18 show. Models wore printed turbans and towels styled as turbans with matching vacation looks. Marc Jacobs brought back the turban as evening wear in his 2018 spring collection, at his show in New York, silk headscarves adorned with brooches and jewels. Turbans were unique variations, some were metallic, coordinating color, and glitter accented, worn with evening gowns and dresses which gave them an edgy look. The turbans milliner Stephen Jones designs, who teamed up with Jacobs for the show.

Also in 2018, Gucci presented men and women in turbans at their fall show in Milan. "The Move" by Alessandro Michele, received conflicting reviews on the turbans being very similar to the religious styles rather than the draped variations.

Cultural and Religious Significance

MORE THAN A WRAP

Turban is highly relevant in many cultures and religions, historically, draped clothing has always been significant in eastern culture. Watson noted,
"Certain strict Hindus still do not wear cut or stitched cloth as for them a garment composed of several pieces sewn together is an abomination and defilement".

Turbans are primarily worn by men and used by women on rare occasions in the past.

"In Vedic literature, Indrani, wife of Indra, wears a headdress known as Usnisa", (Ghuyre).

Some early terms for turban in English were "turban", "tolibanl", and "turband". The French adaptation of the Turkish "tulbend", a vulgarism for the term "dulbend" from Persia, "didband", a scarf or sash wound around the neck.

☐
Turbans in India

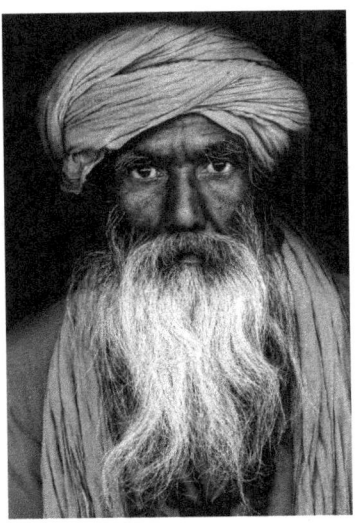

In India, turbans have many local names: "Potia", "usnisa", "pag", "pagri", "safa", and "veshtani". The Sikhs, a community whose followers are dictated to wearing a turban, is called "dastaar".

While the Islamic leaders call it "kalansuwa".

Formally, the turban was commonly made from cotton, then cotton was affordable and abundant, also it is the most comfortable fabric to use in tropical or temperate climates where it was very common. Silk and satin were rare and limited to the affluent and powerful class.

There are specialists called "pagribands" whose skill is in the art of tying the turban and were employed by the erstwhile royalty for their services.

There are innumerable variations of turban, but it can be divided into two types based on size; long turbans and square turban pieces.

The long piece has a length of 7-10meters and a width of 25-100centimeters. The square pieces could be between 1-3meters for each side, with 1-½ meters, constituting the most useful size. There are wide varieties of turbans across different cultures and religions. Distinctions are made based on size, shape, material, color, ornamentation, and method of wrapping.

In the Indian state of Rajasthan, the style of turban very much varies. Rajput turbans are remarkably different from the kind worn in any other region in India, some famous styles are the "Jaipur pagri" and the "Gaj Shahi" turban. The fabric of which is dyed in five distinct colors and was developed by Maharaja Gaj Singh II from the Jodhpur royal family.

In Islam, religious elders often wear a turban wrapped around a cap known in Arabic as a "kalansuwa". These caps come in a spherical or conical shape and this produces variations in the turban shape.

Customs

The turban as a headdress isn't just a fashion statement or cultural paraphernalia, it is symbolic, and it has a meaning beyond the obvious. Turbans serve as an identifier, the wearer can be easily identified as a member of a particular group, tribe, or community, it also serves as an introduction to their cultural, religious, political, and social orientations.

Turbans are significantly associated with the concepts of respect and honor. Sikh men are known to wear a peaked turban, which serves partly as a covering for their hair (which is never cut out of respect for their god). A man's turban is believed to signify his honor and the honor of his people.

The exchanging turbans are considered a sign of everlasting friendship, the exchange signifies a long relationship and forges relationships between families. And gifting someone a turban is considered a great token of esteem. Thus, the turban is an intrinsic part of all ceremonies from birth until death. Conversely, it is considered a grave insult to step over or pick up another man's turban. Turbans are linked intrinsically to the "ego" of a person. To remove a turban and lay it at another's feet symbolizes submission and is an expression of humility.

Turbans convey the social and economic status of the wearer, the season, a festival, a community, and a region. It is also distinguished by the style of wrapping; each fold tells a story. The tightness of the drape, the length of its hanging end, the type of bands created on the surface, say something about its wearer.

Colors

The colors of turbans vary in different cultures and are imbued with complex connotations, emotional context, and rich association. They are used to convey mood, religious values, customs, and ceremonial occasions.

In India, ochre is the color of the saint, saffron denotes chivalry and prosperity. Muslims consider white turbans to be the holiest color, they are used by older men and for mourning, whereas dark blue is reserved for a condolence visit. Among Sikhs of north India, blue and white cotton turbans are considered religious.

In the Middle East, green turbans are considered to be the color of paradise and are worn by men who claim descent from the prophet Muhammad.

The shape and size of the turban are determined by many conditions. The primary conditions are climate, status, and occupation. Turbans that are big and loose without hanging tails used in hot deserts have a protective function. Merchants involved in more sedentary activities tend to wear ornamental turbans with hanging long tails.

Fashionable Wear

In the early 15th century, turbans were introduced into European fashion until the 16th century. It has been revived many times in women's fashion at intervals since the 16th century. Turbans acquired a more contemporary look in the 21st century. Though it still exists in different parts of the world in a more traditional form. Lately, fashion designers and couturiers have adapted to give turbans a more fashionable and chic look, thus making them a popular fashion accessory. Though in their contemporary look turbans may not retain the same symbolism that is attached to their traditional look, but it reinforces the importance of a garment.

CHAPTER 6

THE FUTURE OF HEADWRAP CULTURE IN AFRICA AND THE WORLD AT LARGE (AUTHOR CONCEPTION AND AIM)

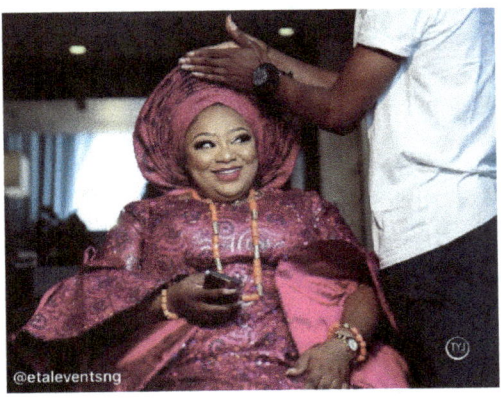

EARLY LIFE

My journey as a Gele stylist started from a very tender age because of my undying love for art, I have so much passion for art most especially drawing and paintings. When I draw oblivious of what is happening around me, one favorite drawing was that of comical superheroes like superman, spider-man, justice league, silver hawk, avatar, and a lot more.

"How did I fall so in love with art?" is a question keep asking myself but I have no clue what the answer is, but I'm settling with that's how God designed me.

Back in my secondary school days, I was one of the best artists in school unfortunately my parent didn't support my artistic gift but as a zealous child, I never stopped drawing it simply because I found pleasure in it. I found expression and solace in drawing, those around me admired my gift and always wanted to be like me. Teachers —majorly my home economics, biology, and fine art teachers - would call on me to draw whenever they needed a drawing or an illustration. Aside from drawing and painting, I loved singing and dancing but I did not harness those potentials until I got to university. My passion for dancing increased because it gave me a sense of iconic feeling.

I studied Theatre and Media Arts, Ekiti State University, Ado-Ekiti (EKSU). I was known as "Flames" in university because I am passionate about anything that has to do with art, which was why I worked on improving my dancing skills, I got a lot of recognition and award. I often helped design the theatrical set alongside the set manager and some colleagues. As a very talented young man, I was often confused about what to do or where to focus on as a career.

As a young entrepreneur and an undergraduate, I faced struggles of managing both school and business, but as time went by I had a lot of time to reason, evaluate, create and also see life in a broader spectrum, which gave me strength. My vision grew stronger with the power of determination, stealth, resilience, and creativity.

HOW IT ALL STARTED

Before my university admission, my mum who is a make-up artist taught me the art of make-up and gele tying, this built my foundation in gele craft. I would make-up and tie geles of people mostly party attenders in other to make little money. This was a source of livelihood to me in my early undergraduate days. But things changed when I learned gele as a skill from a professional.

Professionally, I learned gele craft from one of the best stylists, ONIGELE. Onigele is an inspiration to me. To be candid, meeting him wasn't just on a bargain of obtaining the skill but a path-finding encounter. He is more than my mentor, he isa friend, a helper, a brother, he is practically family. My training was for a few weeks and began to personally improve my skill.

Tying gele became a hobby a day doesn't go by without me wrapping up something, I practiced styles I was taught and created new ones. I named a mannequin 'ANIKE' because she

was always there for me whenever I needed her.
POWER OF THE MIND

During my professional training, I'd always virtualize practicing step by step what I had learned that I couldn't practice at home because training ends late and I'd be stuck in traffic for hours. That played a very vital role in my growth as Gele Stylist. I discovered a secret, 'The Power of the Mind and Imagination'. This made me understand one can achieve whatever he/she wants to all that is needed is first create it in your mind, then physically materialize it. Like when I started the journey of tying gele which wasn't easy but because I saw a future in it, I kept believing that someday it will be a reality.

The mind can be defined as a person's set of intellectual or mental faculties. The human mind refers to the group of cognitive psychiatric processes that includes functions like perception, memory, reasoning (executive functions), etc.

Major cognitive skills that make up our mind:
- Attention: Attention is the ability to choose and concentrate on relevant stimuli. Attention is the cognitive process that makes it possible to position ourselves towards relevant stimuli and consequently respond to them.
- Perception: Perception is the ability to capture, process, and actively make sense of the information that our senses receive. It is the cognitive process that makes it possible to interpret our surroundings with the stimuli that we receive throughout sensory organs.
- Memory: Memory is the brain's ability to retain information and voluntarily recover it when needed. In other words, memory is what makes it possible to remember facts, ideas, feelings, relationships between concepts.
- Reasoning (Executive Functions): Superior cognitive functions, like reasoning, make it possible to relate the information that we perceive with the information that we have stored, which helps hypothesize and resolve problems that arise in daily life.

MORE THAN A WRAP

- Coordination: Coordination is the skill that makes it possible to move efficiently and precisely. It is the mental function responsible for making us efficiently interact with the environment.

The Imagination

Imagination is the ability to produce and simulate novel objects, sensations, and ideas in the mind without any immediate input of the senses.

"Imagination" is one of those words that inspire us. It reminds us of children playing and Einstein claiming that it's more important than knowledge. The word is used in different ways, but for most people, it means one of two things.

First, people use the word to refer to creativity in general — saying that someone has a great imagination or no imagination at all.

Second, people use the word to refer to mental imagery of some kind — either picturing something in your head, like how your childhood bedroom looked or hearing a song in your head to try to recall lyrics.

I'm interested in both kinds of images for the sake of this book.

New Gele Styles As A Product of Imagination

The power of the mind and imagination can't be over-emphasized, simply because as humans, we rely on our superior capabilities and intelligence to survive. Creative art is a product of imagination that is birthed from the mind and the art of Headwrap isn't an exception.

The first gele I invented was the "Ace-Gele", this kick-started my game with fame. This invention went viral on Instagram and Facebook, it brought a lot of curious but purposeful crowd. It was what I needed to start, as I got customers who kept requesting my service. I have invented a series of styles after the Ace-Gele, they are listed below. In the year 2017, I invented the "Auto-Gele" which had over 24,000 views on Instagram and over 1k repost on Facebook. This was a huge success, I had orders rolling in from both home and abroad.

The name "EnnyGeleCraft" was a combination of my nickname "Enny", with "Gele" and "Craft" which when pronounced sounds like "ANY-GELE" craft, which means any style of gele. EnnyGeleCraft as a brand has styled more than a hundred brides and party-guest in Nigeria has also worked with a lot of celebrities.

I, Eniola founder of EnnyGeleCraft has contributed greatly to the growth and advancement of Gele in Nigeria and Africa at large. He invented eight designs of Gele, which are;

☐
1. Ace Gele

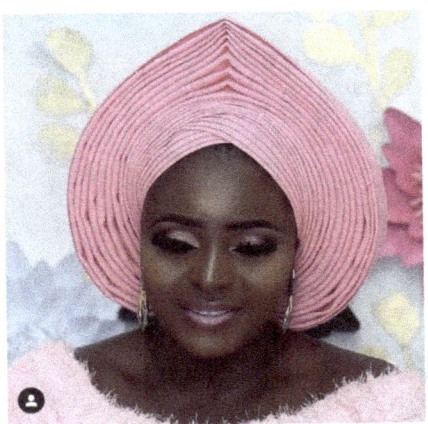

This is a very simple style of Gele which was inspired by an ace logo on my T-shirt. Tying the Ace Gele involves following steadily the step-by-step instructions made available in chapter 7.

2. Arewa Gele

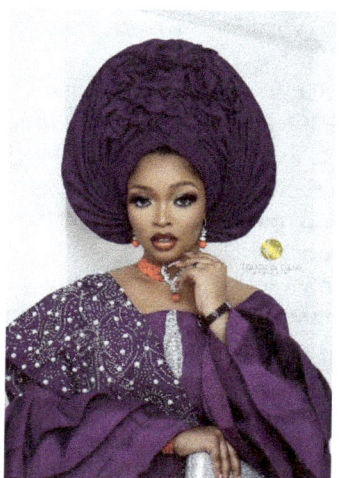

This is a complex Gele that owns up to its name. The Gele is a combination of fans on two sides and ruffles to give a royalty look.

3. Wavy Pleats Gele

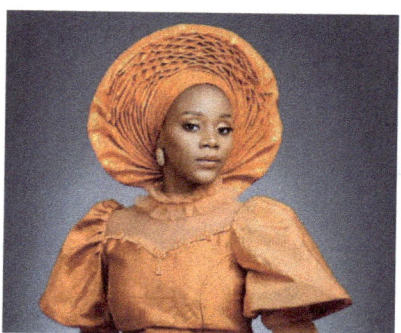

MORE THAN A WRAP

The wavy pleats Gele is very complex because of the diamond-like design in the middle. It's a very beautiful Gele which might require extra effort and time.

4.   Ruffles Gele

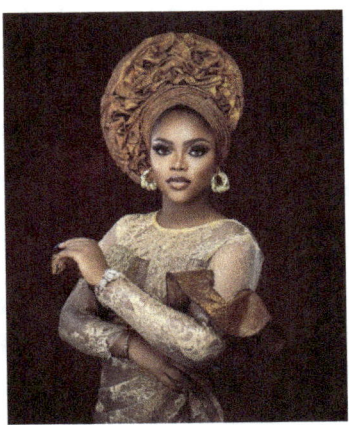

The ruffles Gele is known for its twisted and ruffles-like material which can be tied in different styles. It's a form of Gele styling that can be combined with other styles to create unconventional styles.

5.   Asymmetrical Gele

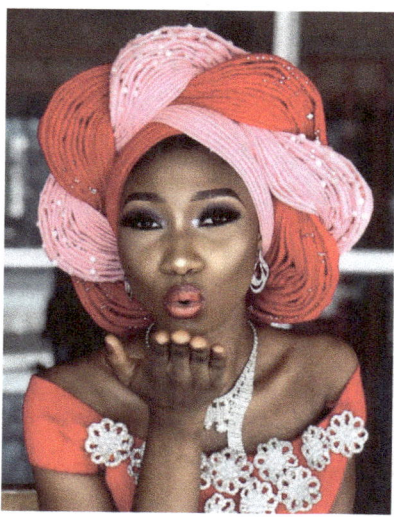

The name of this gele is gotten from its shape which, is called the asymmetrical Gele. It is made using two Gele materials and wrapped up in a symmetrical pattern.

- 6. Apple Gele

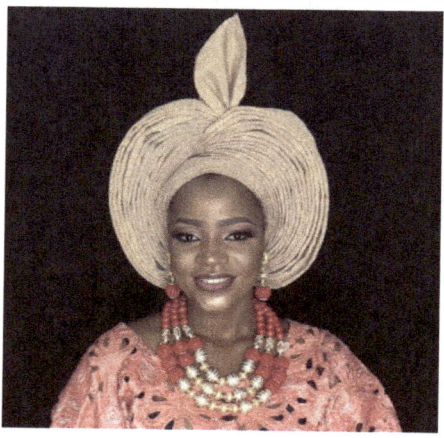

MORE THAN A WRAP

The Apple Gele was inspired by the Apple logo (iPhone). Apple Gele is made to look like an Apple using Asooke fabric.

7. EnnyGeleCraft Facinators.

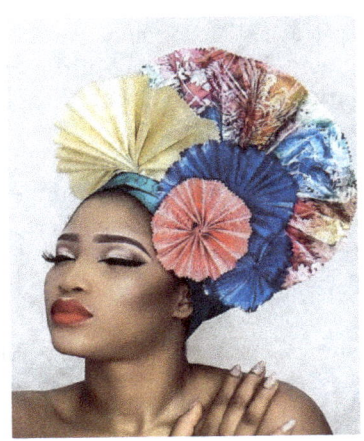

Fascinators are headgears that often look like a hat. It is used to compliment attires. EnnyGeleCraft Fascinators is made from sego fabric with an ornament mix of colors which makes it looks so unique

THE NEXT LEVEL
In the year 2019, EnnyGeleCraft was nominated as part of the designer during an event held in Ekiti State, led by Her

MORE THAN A WRAP

Excellency Erelu Bisi Fayemi, titled "Ekiti Entrepreneurship Week". The event brought about various fashion designers in and out of Ekiti and served as an eye-opener to the potentials and expertise of entrepreneurs in the state. The appearance of celebrities was not exempted as the recognition of international brands and designers were utilized and various fashion designer displayed their beautiful outfits one after the other including EnnyGeleCraft. Aside from the display of skill and professionalism awards, prices and recognitions were given to various outstanding designers. The experience at this event was very valuable, it fired up my zeal. EnnyGeleCraft exhibited the art of gele craft, assisted by the president of "FADAN NIGERIA", the brand was allowed to display its skill by styling geles on stage. EnnyGeleCraft came to the first runner-up and was also given a cash price by Her Excellency herself, also I was invited to be a member of the Fashion Designers Association of Nigeria (FADAN).

As you can see, geles are becoming important elements for exhibitions in fashion shows and pageants. The culture of headwraps is spreading at the speed of light as many fashion enthusiasts imbibe headwrap as a compliment to promote clothing.

Headwraps on Intercontinental Stage

The future of headwrap is not only promising but of such that comes with noticeable and consistent growth in Africa and the world at large. Gele has been seen in major pageant walk shows in Nigeria and the diaspora.

In an article published by Vogue, "Premium scarves, hijabs, turbans, and dupatta all signal a universally, over-arching movement for being covered but in unique, sartorial ways. It's no surprise then that the headgear, whether in the form of an intricately-twisted turban or wrap, consistently emerges as a striking hair accessory on the ready-to-wear and couture runways for Fall 2017 and beyond. In the most recent Marc Jacobs Spring 2018 extravaganza, where models including Bella and Gigi Hadid, Kaia Gerber, and Taylor Hill took to the runway in silk, jewel-encrusted turbans, and scarves worn to one side. Meanwhile, at Jean Paul Gaultier's Fall 2017 Couture show, models sported metallic gold teardrops paired with embellished shawls draped over their heads. Sometimes, scarves are more than just a mere fashion statement. Also serving as a religious accouterment, who can forget when Vogue Arabia cover girl Halima Aden made history as the first hijab-wearing model at the Yeezy Fall 2017 show? In the gallery ahead, we round up the best scarf moments from the runways of Givenchy, Donna Karan, Issa, and more."

In another article, "The headwrap was a brilliant blue. It mirrored the applique on the long yellow bodice of the strapless gown and was echoed in the shoes and handbag. Lupita Nyong'o wore the outfit this past week at the Toronto premiere of her film Queen of Katwe. Fashion critics called it "flawless."

Fashion queen Carolina Herrera was the designer of that dress, she was born in Venezuela and now living in America. But the head tie is pure Nigerian. That got Nigerians buzzing, not necessarily in admiration.

If you want gele tying, there are over 859,000 how-to tie gele videos on YouTube. It's a testimony to the intercontinental and international reach of Nigerian fashion, spurred by a growing entertainment industry and a renaissance in art and culture on the continent.

THE FUTURE

As a Professional Gele stylist, I intend to celebrate, promote and ensure the continued existence and growth of Headwrap not only in Nigeria but in Africa at large. And to do that, I'm working on creating a global Professional Headgear stylist community. In this digitized world, where businesses, sales, education, and so on can be established and maintained over the internet. I intend to create an online platform centralized on the services of styling Gele by experts, through this online platform customers can request a stylist anywhere in the world.

CHAPTER 7

HOW TO BE AN EXCEPTIONAL GELE STYLIST/ WORKSHOP

7 Secrets to Being an Exceptional Gele Stylist/ Workshop

1. Concept of mastery
2. Mystics of creativity
3. Competence and composure
4. Precision
5. Patience and tolerance
6. Humility
7. Customer management

1. Concept of mastery: Life is like a game of chess, to win you have to make a move. Knowing which move to make comes with insight and knowledge, and by learning through experience along the way to success, we become each piece that forms the whole picture. Robert Greene once said, "mastery is not a function of genius or talent. It is a function of time and intense focus applied to a particular field of knowledge." Headwrap crafting can be likened to every other form of craft which requires a certain level of commitment and practice in other to attain the perfection of such craft. The secret of being exceptional in any field comes with the sacrifice which is mostly measured in time and effort. Gele styling requires a lot of practice which enables the trainee to understand and form a cordial relationship with both the craft and fabric used. With practice comes mastery, with mastery comes knowledge, with knowledge comes strength.

2. Mystics of creativity: Skill is power but the ability to

create is even more powerful. The power of creativity cannot be over-emphasized as there is no doubt that creativity is the most important human resource. Without creativity, there would be no progress and we would be forever repeating the same pattern. According to Wikipedia, "creativity is a phenomenon whereby something somehow new and somehow valuable is formed. It can as well be seen as the ability to create or recognize ideas, alternative, or useful possibilities". In the world today where innovations and inventions take their toll, advancing the culture and the quality of life. It is pivotal for a gele stylist to ensure he harnesses the creative potential thereby breaking limits and setting new standards.

3. Competence and composure: The efficiency or performance of a skill or job is solely based on the level of competency an individual exhibits. Competence is a combination of practical and cognitive skills, behavior, values which is applied to improve performance in a particular field. Competency and composure are significant and propel one another. As a gele stylist, one of the important secrets to thrive is competency coupled with a composed attitude and mindset as this will enable sustain the boldness to create and deal with customers in general.

4. Precision: The accuracy or exactness through a process, procedure, or pattern being reenacted is known as precision. Precision helps to add professionalism and glamour to a person (gele styles). Therefore, in other to stand out as a headgear stylist one needs to ensure accuracy and exactness while styling a particular style of gele. The confidence of a headgear stylist lies in how well he can create his art on a customer's head thereby earning the trust and loyalty of such customer.

5. Patience and tolerance: Patience is not the ability to wait but the ability to keep a good attitude while waiting. There is a popular assertion that says, "one minute of patience, ten

years of peace. Patience is a virtue that isn't common but whoever can exercise it such a person would attain greatness. Tolerance is the ability to endure during a particular situation or person even when it isn't convenient. Both patience and tolerance are inseparable in this context a headgear stylist needs to ensure he equips himself with this quality. For example; for a customer who is unpredictable or isn't easily satisfied, to deal with such a customer one needs to apply patience and tolerance in other to sustain the longevity of the relationship between the two parties.

6. Humility: According to Saint Vincent De Paul, "humility is nothing but the truth and, pride is nothing but lies". Nothing makes way for a person quicker and faster than humility. The act of humility is rare in the world today as more people become boastful and proud due to their status or achievement. There is dignity and greatness in being humble. In the book of James 4:6, "God opposes the proud but gives grace to the humble". Also in Philippians 2:3-4, "Do nothing from selfish ambition or conceit, but in humility count others more significant than yourselves. Let each of you look not only to his interests but also to the interests of others.

7. Customer management: The longevity of a business is based on a healthy relationship between services providers and customers. Sustaining the ability to earn, maintain and retain a customer is not common around us and that is why a lot of business don't go too far and also fails at attaining success. The relationship between the customer and the headgear stylist is therefore important in the growth of a business as a customer would only reproduce more customers through referral.

THE ART OF STYLING GELE

The art of tying gele is stylish, an art that compels admiration with ease. Admittedly, a gele that is skillfully tied evokes a certain kind of beauty; the kind that can only be seen among the beautiful people of Africa.

How to tie gele fabrics has been the agitation of most Nigerian women recently because it exploded creativity and the revamped touch had made gele gotten the attention of millions of people in different countries all over the world. Many non-Africans wear gele as a sign of reverence when attending African events, some as a part of their everyday life wear and some that have gotten a soft spot for the Yoruba Culture. Therefore, tying gele has become a modern statement for today's complete traditional look and it makes waves all around the world.

Gele comes in different forms and they are classified based on the type of fabric with the overall fitting look. For the renowned gele that has become a fad especially at weddings and other events, it's necessary to be able to tie it in a modern and classy way without fuss. African Women can be very particular on how they want their gele tied.

Some like them tied in levels to stand high while some like them tied in a more conservative way. However, gele length can range from 8" wide and 54" Long for African Print, while 34" wide and 72" Long for Gele Paper-like Head-tie, down to 20" wide and 80" long for Aso-Oke.

Many people have this wrong notion that gele is a head-tie is used to only wedding parties. Permit me to change your perception, I have laid out a step by step methods of tying both normal and modern gele. However, according to experts, it takes a good sense of skill to properly tie the gele; and that skill is not easy to cultivate. But, in any case, you can do it yourself if you practice with the following steps.

THE PROCESS

Before tying a gele some basic important factors to be considered, there are;
1. The type of material in use (quality, texture, and design)

2. The length of the material
3. The intended style of Gele
4. The head shape of the muse
5. The measurement of the style involves a formula

All factors are much important and should be thoroughly adhered to in other to achieve the proposed style perfectly.

TYPE OF MATERIALS

We have three major types of materials in Nigeria which are used to tie gele, which are;
- Asooke
- Sego
- Ankara

Asooke

Aso-Oke is the short version of the more formal "Aso Ilu Oke" which roughly translates to 'clothes from the up-country'. It is the traditional wear of the Yoruba tribe, the second largest tribe found in the southwestern part of Nigeria. They are and Aso-oke is often worn as a celebration cloth on special occasions and important events.

Aso-oke is a special hand-woven cloth, the method of making aso-ebi is painstaking. The threads used to weave the material are made out of cotton planted during the rainy season between June and July. By November and as late as January, the cotton is ready to be harvested.

PROCESS OF ASOOKE MAKING

The cotton is then spun to separate the cottonseed from wool and a spindle, known in Yoruba as 'Orun', is used to achieve this. The weaver spreads the wool and processes it through the loom. As the spindle turns repeatedly, the cotton thins this is done until all the wool has been spun. The cotton is then cleaned and sorted which is done manually and can be very time-consuming.

Once the cotton is purified, designs and patterns

characteristic of Aso-oke are ready to be created. The designs and patterns are made on the Aso-Oke while the cloth is being woven. During the pattern process, cotton reels are hung upon the hangers on the sets of metallic pegs on the ground. After everything has been prepared, the weaving can begin.

The weaving, quite possibly the most important part of the process, is a delicate process. The weaver deftly presses down on the pedals of the orun and hands are used to weave the material to create designs in a variety of colors. The entire process of creating Aso-Oke is a beautiful sight and seeing artisans who have spent long hours perfecting their craft make it so effortlessly is heart-warming. Watching plain cotton transform into perfectly woven threads is a testament to the craftsmanship we are capable of in Africa.

In recent years, asooke making has evolved as the art of weaving the fabric has developed into creating various designs and pattern some of which are;

- Two-tone asooke
- Multicolored
- Grantex
- Super net
- Sequentially beaded asooke

SEGO

Sego which is also called 'paper gele' is an imported design of gele that is mostly used by the Igbo tribe in Nigeria. This type of gele is a rigid one that requires a certain level of skill and expertise in handling.

Sego comes in various designs, lengths, patterns, and also in various attractive colors and embellishments. it is made out of net-like material which is tightly weaved together unlike the asooke fabric which is made out of cotton and sometimes a mixture of the net.

The south-eastern part of Nigeria especially Benin, Warri, port-Harcourt, Bayelsa, etc. Are popularly known for wearing large elaborate gele as a compliment to their attire. Some of the ceremonial events of which they are worn are Weddings, chieftaincy, burials, etc. The most popular style which sego gele is major used for is "fan gele". The procedure of how to tie one can be seen below.

ANKARA

The Ankara fabric is one of the most popular fabrics in Nigeria. African prints textile is made with the Ankara that is also referred to as 'African wax prints', 'Holland wax', or 'Dutch wax'. The Ankara fabric is generally known for its colorful African prints and is deeply associated with African clothing. One of the alluring things about Ankara fabric is the intensity of its African prints does not change compared to other printed textiles that fade quickly. This is because of the "wax resistant" technique used in printing the textile.

The method of producing African print fabric is called batik, where designs are printed onto the cloth using wax before using dye. You'll notice the crackling effect on the African textile, and it is caused by the wax-resist dyeing technique. His company, Vlisco, introduced the printed textile to Ghana, and the fabric has gained an African identity.

Ankara fabric can be handmade or produced on large-scale textile machines. The handmade African print Ankara is unique and has varieties of patterns. On the other hand, machine-made Ankara typically has imperfections or a "crackling" effect.

In 1846, there was a high demand for printed cotton, so Dutch entrepreneur Pieter Fentener Van Vlissingen mechanized the method used to make prints on batiks—a popular cloth worn in Indonesia. African textile that is known as 'Kitenge' in East Africa and 'Ankara' in West Africa was first produced in Indonesia.

THE LENGTH OF MATERIAL

One of the major factors to consider before tying a gele is the length of the material. In achieving a certain style, a certain length is needed and compulsory. The length of a material varies depending on the type of fabric and can be sometimes

determined by an individual. Some of the fabrics and measurements are;
- Asooke: this fabric comes in different measures most times according to individual preferences which are namely;
  - 2yards
  - 2quater
  - 2half

- Sego: this fabric due to its production style which is industrial comes with a particular measurement and most times can't be changed by an individual.

- Ankara: this fabric comes in enormous length and width which according to individual preference can be purchased or adjusted.

The length of material is pivotal to the achieving of a certain style of gele. Furthermore, the stylist should ensure to confirm the length of a gele before the further procedure.

INTENDING TO STYLE?

Styling gele entails a lot of procedures which is the foresight of creation. Before styling a gele the stylist needs to be put in consideration two things.

Head Shape of Muse: The other important thing to note is the head shape of the muse. The head shape predetermination the fitting of the gele on the head of the carrier. We have different types of head shapes some of which are; oblong, circle, diamond, oval, heart-shaped, inverted triangle, rectangle, etc.

The Measurement of The Style Which Requires a Formula: One of the most complex procedures in tying gele is how to achieve the correct measurement before styling commence. A lot of apprentice struggle with the process due to some of the needed mathematical apprehension. Each type of gele has its various measuring formula and length which is contained in the table below.

STYLES	LENGTH	FORMULA
Advance Bridal Round	2quarter	45 - 55
(Billion pleat round)	2half	
Bridal Fan Gele	2quarter	45 - 55
	2half	
Perfect Full-Fan Gele	2yards	25 - 75
	2quarter	30 - 70
	2half	35 - 65
Avante Garde	''' ''''	10 - 90

HOW TO TIE MODERN GELE STYLES

Advance Bridal Round Gele

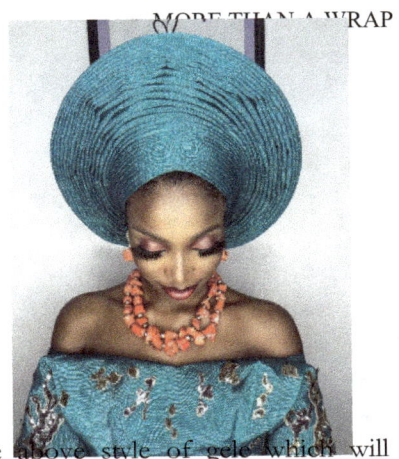

The above style of gele which will be treated is called Advanced bridal round gele (billion pleats), it can be a tie with either Aso-oke or Ankara fabric materials. They usually look beautiful in and out.

PROCEDURE:

Step 1: It is important that you ensure your gele has a perfect and solid foundation for a perfect gele, remember that the beauty of the gele lies in the perfect, neat, and clean look you are expected to have at the end of the process. So you need to start the process by folding at the end of the gele, this will help the gele fabrics to have a smooth base at the front.

Step 2: Measure your gele length (2yards, 2quarter, 2half)

Step 3: Apply the formula to achieve your selected style.

Step 3: Base your foundation by picking your base pleat.

Step 4: Continue with the process by picking your follow-through pleat which is a billion pleats that form the major part of the gele.

Step 5: knot your gele twice and pin when necessary.

Bridal Fan Gele

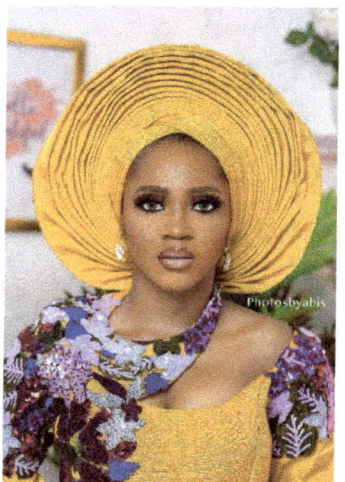

The bridal fan is a style of gele that has a mixture of two different variations which is both round and fan. It is a style that has been popular for a long and has now been developed to look even more fascinating and elegant.

PROCEDURE:

Step 1. It is important that you ensure your gele have a perfect and solid foundation for a perfect gele, remember that the beauty of the gele lies in the perfect, neat, and clean look you are expected to have at the end of the process. So you need to start the process by folding at the end of the gele, this will help the gele fabrics to have a smooth base at the front.

Step 2: Measure your gele length (2yards, 2quarter, 2half)

Step 3: Apply the formula to achieve your selected style.

Step 3: Base your foundation by picking your base pleat.

Step 4: Continue with the process by picking your follow-through pleats which is the pleat that forms the style/major part of the gele.

Step 5: knot your gele twice and pin when necessary.

Perfect

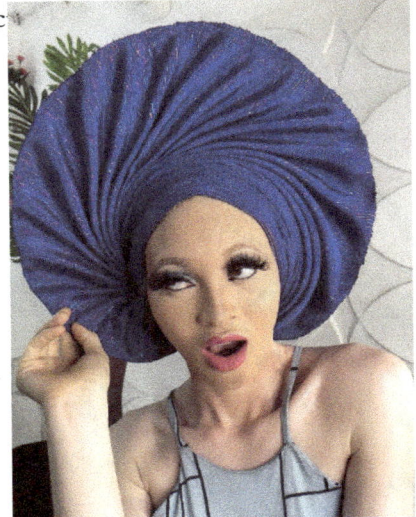

Full fan gele is an elaborate-looking gele that gives a sense of royalty to the wearer. The specifically associated with the Igbo tribe and tied mostly with the sego material. Asooke can also be used to achieve this style.

PROCEDURE:

Step 1. It is important that you ensure your gele have a perfect and solid foundation for a perfect gele, remember that the beauty of the gele lies in the perfect, neat, and clean look you are expected to have at the end of the process. So you need to start the process by folding at the end of the gele, this will help the gele fabrics to have a smooth base at the front.

Step 2: Measure your gele length (2yards, 2quarter, 2half)

Step 3: Apply the formula to achieve your selected style.

Step 3: Base your foundation by picking your base pleat.

Step 4: Continue with the process by picking your follow-through pleats (fan pleats) which is the pleat that forms the style/major part of the gele.

Step 5: knot your gele twice and pin when necessary.

Avante Garde

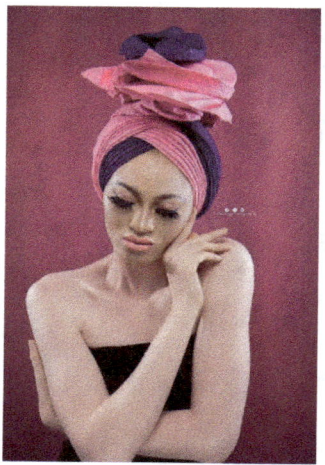

Avante Garde is an iconic style of gele which goes with just any attire. This style of gele is famous for its appearance on Run-way pergeant walk shows.

PROCEDURE:

Step 1. It important that you ensure your gele have a perfect and solid foundation for a perfect gele, remember that the beauty of the gele lies in the perfect, neat and clean look you are expected to have at the end of the process. So you need to start the process by folding in the end of the gele, this will help the gele fabrics to have a smooth base at the front.

Step 2: Measure your gele length (2yards, 2quarter, 2half)

Step 3: Apply the formula to achieving your selected style.

Step 3: Base your foundation by picking your base pleat.

Step 4: Continue with process by picking your follow through pleat which is the pleat that form the style/major part of the gele.

Step 5: Ensure you pin correctly to avoid accidental unwrap.

MORE THAN A WRAP

For visual and practicality of all styles, visit our YouTube Channel, @Ennygelecraft TM. Don't forget to like and Subscribe.

REFERENCES.

https://www.ashro.com/blog/headwrap/headwraps-101/

https://www.nationalclothing.org/africa/256-a-short-history-of-african-headwrap.html

https://www.sexysicklecell.org/headwraptransition/

https://www.fashion-history.lovetoknow.com/fashion-accessories/turban

https://www.aeworld.com/fashion/fashion-women/your-comprehensive-history-of-a-turban/

https://www.south world.net/the-african-head-scarf-a-work-of-art/

https://www.thewrap.life/blogs/journal/can-you-wear-headwraps

https://aphrochic.com/2017/05/15/Headwrap-a-cultural-symbol/

https://www.asikarabylaurajane.co.ku/post/headwraphistory1

https://www.oleoduduwa.com/yoruba-head-wrap-gele/

https://www.en.m.wikipedia.org/wiki/Head_tie

https://www.empiretextiles.com/products/Head-Gear/

https://www.naturallycurly.com/curlreading/hairstyles/the-history-of-headwraps-then-there-and-now

https://www.plato.Stanford.edu/entries/aesthetic-concept/

https://www.google.com/amp/s/the conversation.com/amp/nigerias-tradition-of-matching-outfits-at-events-has-a-downside-131235

https://www.blog.swaliafrica.com/owanbe-in-the-spirit-of-celebration/

https://www.researchgate.net/publication/328530889_clothing_as_medium_of_communication

https://www.jpanafrican.org/docs/vo/5no6/5.7-AAso%20Ebi.pdf

https://www.clothetrotter.wixsite.com/clothetrotter/single-post/2017/04/26/the-history-of-the-head-wrap

https://www.google.com/amp/s/www.amplifyafrica.org/amp/tignon-law-policing-black-women-s-hair-in-the-18th-century

https://timeline.com/headwraps-were-born-out-of-slavery-before-being-reclaimed-207e2c65703b?gi=aa07932989b7

https://www.duraggy.com/blog/historyofdurags

https://fashion-history.lovetoknow.com/fashion-accessories/turban

https://www.encyclopedia.com/sports-and-everyday-life/fashion-and-clothing/clothing-jewelry-and-personal-adornment/turbans

https://www.google.com/amp/s/bellatory.com/.amp/fashion-accessories/Nigerian-Women-and-Their-Gele

https://study.com/academy/lesson/egyptian-headdress-history-meaning-facts.html

https://www.google.com/amp/s/www.vice.com/amp/en/article/j5abvx/black-womens-hair-illegal-tignon-laws-new-orleans-louisiana

https://jiji-blog.com/2017/09/gele-tying/

https://plato.stanford.edu/entries/art-definition/

https://courses.lumenlearning.com/boundless-arthistory/chapter/what-is-art/

https://www.cognifit.com/mind

https://en.m.wikipedia.org/wiki/Imagination

https://www.google.com/amp/s/en.vogue.me/fashion/10-times-scarves-turned-heads-on-the-runway/amp/

https://concise.ng/how-to-tie-gele/

https://www.oludan.com/blogs/news/a-brief-history-of-ankara-fabric-and-african-prints

ABOUT THE AUTHOR

Fatola Eniola is a professional headwrap stylist who owns an award-winning brand 'Ennygelecraft'. A bachelor of arts degree holder and a master of his craft. This book contains wealth of knowledge which readers should dive into without hesitations. "MORE THAN A WRAP", is my first book as an author and I urge readers to expect more interesting and educative books from me.

www.ingramcontent.com/pod-product-compliance
Lightning Source LLC
Chambersburg PA
CBHW070253220526
45465CB00004B/1599